DEAR DAMAGE

DEAR DAMAGE

ASHLEY MARIE FARMER

SARABANDE BOOKS Louisville, KY

Dear Damage is a work of nonfiction. Certain names and details
have been changed or omitted to protect identities. While some
conversations may be compressed or recreated, I have done my
best to convey these events accurately based on public information,
media, recordings, conversations with family, and memory.

Publisher's Cataloging-In-Publication Data
(Prepared by The Donohue Group, Inc.)

Names: Farmer, Ashley F., author.
Title: Dear Damage / Ashley Marie Farmer.
Description: Louisville, KY : Sarabande Books, 2022
Includes bibliographical references.
Identifiers: ISBN 9781946448903 (paperback)
ISBN 9781946448910 (e-book)
Subjects: LCSH: Farmer, Ashley F.—Family. | Grandparents.
Paralytics—Death. | Mariticide. | LCGFT: Essays.
Classification: LCC PS3606.A7138 D43 2022 (print)
LCC PS3606.A7138 (e-book) | DDC 814/.6—dc23

Cover and interior design by Alban Fischer.
Printed in Canada.
This book is printed on acid-free paper.
Sarabande Books is a nonprofit literary organization.

   [clmp]

This project is supported in part by an award from the National
Endowment for the Arts. The Kentucky Arts Council, the state
arts agency, supports Sarabande Books with state tax dollars and
federal funding from the National Endowment for the Arts.

For Cindy Lynn

CONTENTS

The mercy of the world is you don't know what's going to happen.

—WENDELL BERRY, *Jayber Crow*

It was the light in things that made them last.

—DAVID BERMAN, "Governors on Sominex"

ONE

MERCY

On January 19, 2014, my grandfather Bill walked into my grand-mother Frances's hospital room with a loaded gun he'd purchased that morning. He set their Neptune Society cards side by side on a nearby table and kissed his sleeping wife of sixty-three years. Then he shot her once in the chest. He tried to shoot himself, too, but a spring popped from the pawn shop gun and the weapon broke apart in his hands. Correctional officers who were at the Carson City, Nevada, hospital that day arrested him. According to subsequent news stories, he wept as he was apprehended. "I failed in my mission," he said.

Sun dotted my Long Beach, California, apartment as my sister relayed this news over the phone. I'd been grading student essays on a weirdly warm winter morning, and now my brain flickered, and it felt like a hand had my throat. I interrupted her to tell my husband, Ryan, what happened—"My grandpa shot my grandma and now he's in jail and she might die"—and then shock propelled us: we slipped on our shoes and walked quick miles down Ocean Boulevard with the sea shimmering below us. I thought of the people in the hospital who heard the gunshot, how horrified and panicked they must've felt, and then the word *ruined* echoed in my brain, a powerful certainty that everything good about our close-knit family was finished. My grandmother shot, my grandfather in jail: these two people I love so much and know so well now shattering—and my mom, who lived with them both, left to pick up the pieces.

Ryan and I shared an American Spirit on a park bench—I wasn't even a smoker—and I took my shoes off and stood on the shore where the tide washed over my toes. The sand looked tiger-striped and glittered with flecks of mica, and I thought about how many times Frances, who was born and raised in Los Angeles, swam in this same ocean or, years later, depicted it in dramatic oil seascapes I've memorized. I figured I should be exactly there, feet freezing in the water, when someone inevitably delivered the news that she'd passed. But amid the flurry of phone calls from my siblings and mom who now drove to the hospital, news of Frances's death didn't arrive: doctors declared that she wouldn't survive her injury, but it could be hours before she left us, days.

When we returned from the beach, my students' essays on the American Dream sat where I'd left them, a collection of sunny, abstract relics from just a few hours ago, the era of before, not after. I couldn't focus enough to make sense of their words, and maybe words would never make sense again. *Gun?* I thought. *Shot?* I thought. *Ruined.* Surely this cataclysm must be a mistake and this nausea gripping me must belong to someone else.

I Googled *Carson City shooting*: news crews already filmed in front of the hospital crime scene tape—a violent tableau that somehow belonged to us. At a different link: footage of my siblings' backs as they rushed toward the entrance. Other news outlets reported from the jail where they now had my grandfather on suicide watch. In yet another piece I'd view hours later, a woman held a microphone outside my grandparents' home, the home that belongs to all of us, the site of Christmas dinners and sagebrush Easter egg hunts, the house my grandpa built by hand, the one we picked out moss-covered rocks for from the old mine. The house where you'll find us grandkids' names scratched into concrete

4

beside our small handprints. Where my grandparents' initials are ringed with a heart in Frances's perfect script—an image the cameraman came close enough to film.

✦

This isn't a story I often share. I've feared others' judgements, and I become flooded with the temptation to explain—we're not gun people and my grandparents are more than just grandparents and, and, and. . . . Plus, despite the public nature of this event and the fact that strangers have dissected it in their own articles and posts, I've wondered which parts are mine to tell. There's also this: the few times I've shared it—with a coworker, a stranger, an old friend over a beer at a writing conference—I've watched their faces tense, grimace, wince. Even if I offer a warning or soften it, a story like this can, for the briefest moment, drop an anvil on a listener. And I've decided in these past few years that if there's one thing I don't want to do, it's contribute more pain to the world.

Instead, I've made a quiet study of pain, the blinding, bewildering strain you don't see coming, the pain of reality biting the dust, of looking toward the horizon to see pain extending forever into the future, an unforgiving desert. Or maybe pain has made a study of me, taking up residence in my body, thrumming in my chest, skyrocketing my blood pressure to ER levels and throttling me from sleep at two a.m. until night eases and the sun slides up. Because there's grief, yes, but it's complicated, too: What do you do with pain caused by someone you love, for actions you don't agree with but, on some level, understand? For a gunshot—a gunshot in public, no less—in a time of mass shootings? For my suffering grandmother? For my weeping grandfather who tried, but failed, to leave us and was now condemned to live?

This disorienting grief proved to be a baptism of sorts: even though I've barely been to church, I found myself in the months afterward praying in LA freeway traffic on my way to teach, tossing up pleas of *no more tragedy* to clouds or smog as I sailed between adjunct gigs. And if begging couldn't change the circumstances, I figured I could at least find the sterling takeaway, a thesis statement with supporting evidence leading up to a tidy "In conclusion..." like I'd find in a student's semester-end reflection essay. I wanted to make sense of not only my grandfather's actions and the ramifications, but also of pain itself because pain, after all, was not only the result but also the cause.

See, two weeks before my grandfather bought the gun, my grandmother tripped as she walked across their living room. It was a swift accident on an ordinary day when she'd just shared a late lunch at Katie's Country Kitchen in Minden, Nevada, with my grandfather and my mother and stepfather, Cindy and Earnhardt. It's the kind of thing that could happen to any of us moving quickly across a room on a winter afternoon except, in Frances's case, her body crashed in the most devastating way possible: her chin hit the floor and her neck essentially broke. A freak thing, as they say.

"I'm paralyzed, aren't I?" she asked my mom after paramedics wheeled her down an ER hallway where they'd wait for hours, other emergencies whizzing past them.

"I hope not," my mom said. Then she leaned over her mother's chest and sobbed.

Doctors later compared the damage in my grandmother's neck to that of a victim of a motorcycle wreck. In the weeks that followed, her condition didn't improve. She had, in fact, been especially unlucky: not only was she now quadriplegic—a life-altering condition that occurred in an instant—but she experienced a type of neuropathy that causes an unrelenting pain that the strongest drugs don't touch. Doctors weighed options. While they did, my mom tended to Frances by rubbing lavender lotion into her feet, by applying Frances's makeup the way she wore it, by dripping drops of Starbucks onto her tongue since Frances could no longer eat or drink. The family rallied, hovered. Frances slurred to me over the phone the lie that she was "getting better every day, in every way."

Finally, doctors convened to deliver the grimmest prognosis: there would be no surgery, no healing, no returning to her living room to pick up where the strange day of the accident left off. This would be her new life instead. But in a nursing home. In perpetuity.

"I want to die," Frances pleaded more than once. To my mother, with whom she shares a birthday, the two of them stitched together, best friends. To my grandfather, always her anchor. "I want to turn the corner," she pleaded.

And for those reasons, Bill, my quiet, Navy veteran grandpa who'd whistle as he made coffee before anyone else was awake each morning—the most practical, rational guy I've known—said a word to no one about his plan, ate a sit-down breakfast that Earnhardt had prepared, and left to purchase a gun. Then he drove to the hospital with the weapon while families hiked near Lake Tahoe, brunched at noisy casino buffets, prayed at church. A "mercy killing" the reports months later declared.

✦

What can I do with this narrative of suffering? It's less than straightforward, a kaleidoscope of surreal moments from a movie I don't recognize. It involves us viewing my grandfather's televised arraignment, him reading a novel under the jail psychiatrist's cautious eyes before being released on bail late one night. It involves me hugging him in the kitchen the morning after, then sitting in the porch sun together before he gifts me Frances's wedding ring, him remarking that my gray-and-black striped dress matches his mug shot attire. It involves my mom declining to speak with politicians and network news shows that call the landline in the wake of high-profile assisted suicide cases. It involves me writing a note in support of my grandfather to the public defender and being surprised to see my words later quoted in newspaper articles, discussed in opposing ways by people who either support or condemn my grandfather's actions.

Beyond the personal? I've had five years to consider that morning within a broader context: right-to-die laws, violence and privilege, the US healthcare system, the US gun system, the way we collectively view aging, the way we grapple with suffering, the way people engage in comment sections without knowing the nuances of a story or realizing that families might read every remark.

But my hands are empty: five years later, no sparkling realization, no rock-solid thesis. My grandparents are both gone now, and I'm not the person in that Long Beach living room anymore: the shock has long lifted and California is a speck behind me. Yet part of me still stands at the edge of the Pacific with my feet in the surf—still pauses on that tiger-striped beach knowing that, like the tide, more pain will eventually come. It's human and inevitable.

Knowing that simple truth has reshaped my DNA. At a moment when the facts of our world compel us to sharpen ourselves each morning, I'm simultaneously more aware of the softness of others, their sore spots and shadows, the stories they don't spill when we share an airplane row or elevator. I've paradoxically become less afraid of tragedy by knowing that there's nothing you can do to stop it from demolishing a January morning. And, as anyone who's been changed by grief can attest, clichés take on surprising truth: for me, it's that one about every person fighting a private battle. It's the kind of line I'd have spotted in a former student's essay, a sentence I'd have circled in green pen. "Cliché?" I might have scribbled, a question mark to temper the judgment. But here I am, writing it. Both easing up on others and loosening my grip.

In conclusion, I have no conclusion, except this: while I'm skeptical about mining beauty from pain (Frances certainly didn't find her pain beautiful) or landing on a diamond takeaway or even claiming good can come from it, I've learned that time-freezing anguish makes for micro-moments of unexpected reverence. Even when grief scrambles the big picture and clarity remains decades—or maybe forever—out of reach, the particulars come into focus. Like my sister's voice that first day, her voice identical to mine, and the care in it as she relayed terrible news. My mother dripping coffee onto her own mother's tongue. How, in those first days when our family paced my grandparents' house, sick and sleepless and shocked to our marrow, strangers left meals wrapped in cellophane on that same front stoop next to my grandparents' initials. One time, a card and carnations. One time, a bottle of wine like a sacrament. Holy, these details, even to me, a heathen fumbling prayers on the 405.

The tide comes for each of us, the phone call we can't predict, the suffering that refuses comprehension, the moment we're waiting for without knowing it. But there's still sand beneath our feet. And those tiny, glimmering flecks, as unexpected as gold.

JOBS PEAK, 1985

It's a wonder you learned to walk, Frances told me—they carried me everywhere. First baby. In the beginning, we lived together: my mother and father, my grandmother and grandfather, my sweet teenage aunt asleep on the sofa bed, no bedroom. The small house Bill built with his hammer in the sun. They'd left Los Angeles for pine nut hills and the Sierra Nevada, Jobs Peak at the center. I didn't know Job. Our life looked trialless: some mornings, wild horses grazed a small patch of grass and we'd watch from the window, cereal soggy in our bowls. We dried laundry on the line. We parked at lakes and waited for trout to bite. I kissed the orange Avon lip balm off the girl down the road, built sagebrush shelters with the boys. My mom had babies and babysat others while my dad delivered packages: we took a first-day photo, his posture straight, pastel balloons and a homemade banner behind him. He'd hitchhiked west at seventeen with nothing—now a job, a uniform, the start of a family. Even then, I sensed my young parents' effort in making themselves, us, a life, the stakes high, both of them earnest and headstrong. I tried at school, memorized my spelling words, sat up straight in my braid the way they tell girls to, taller than my peers and bored by paperwork like a secretary with a dark imagination. Trespassers Will Be Prosecuted read a sign at a house near my bus stop. I confused *prosecuted* with *executed* and pictured a man with a rifle waiting for me to make the wrong move. I hoped when people died there'd be cottonwoods like the lone one my grandfather had planted. *Please let it be green there,* I thought. Out back, I broke marigold buds and held grasshoppers from mint along the fence. Their bodies made of math, their giant eyes. We didn't go to church and I'd never been baptized, but I wanted to know that there's more than what we forge in this life. Like a heaven with trees when we die. Why do I write this?

DECEMBER 31, 2013

ASHLEY FARMER: Where were you born?

FRANCES DRESSER: Los Angeles.

AF: And where did you go to school?

FD: Franklin High School.

AF: Do you know your address?

FD: 2249 Carlyle Place.

BILL DRESSER: Are you writing this? Is this taking it down?

AF: It's recording it, yeah. So what I'm trying to do is write about California and what it's like to be there right now. You know, it's all kind of strange to me. It's kind of overwhelming, even. But I think a lot about how it was when you were there. Which was a lot different, I would think.

FD: Yes.

AF: If you think back about places you liked to hang out at as a kid, or you liked to visit, or that stick out in your memory: What are some things that you thought were neat about California?

FD: Exposition Park.

AF: Where's that?

FD: It's in LA. And it has a museum there. And . . . what else does it have there?

BD: They had places where you could play in the water. It wasn't like a pool but . . .

FD: A little pond.

BD: Do you remember that?

FD: No [*laughs*].

AF: What else? Where else did you guys go?

FD: The beach, for me.

AF: What beach would that be?

BD: Venice.

FD: Venice.

AF: Both of you, Venice?

FD: He went to Venice a lot, me just when I could get out of the house [*laughs*].

BD: And I went to Venice High School.

AF: And you were born in Torrance?

BD: Los Angeles. And there weren't any freeways back then.

FD: So it was a longer drive.

BD: Yep.

FD: A matter of fact, it was so long, the closer we got to the ocean, I could smell it. We'd go like, "Oh, I can smell the ocean!"

AF: And you remember, too, what the landscape looked like before it was all freeway?

BD: There were lots of orange trees and everybody had fruit trees. Back then we had incinerators that we burned our trash in.

AF: I just read about that in a book I taught and how they thought that was the best way until they realized it was polluting things.

BD: We didn't have smog back then.

FD: It wasn't as crowded, you know. There weren't as many people.

BD: The first time we had smog was when we started protecting the orange groves with . . .

FD: Smudge pots. They'd light those up and it would make a lot of smog all over the orange groves so the fruit wouldn't freeze.

I've even heard it to this day that it was a mistake taking the streetcars out.

BD: Oh yeah, yeah. Is it going alright?

AF: Yep. It's working. We're recording.

AFTERMATH

In the aftermath of Frances's death, I fly to Nevada. I want to make sense of what happened, but there's no chance of that. Instead, my sister and I race into the cheap chain store that stays open all night. We float like ghosts in leggings and winter coats, Mallory and I, our eyes bleary and faces drawn, me taller and older, her smaller and younger, eight years between us, but twins in our days-old grief.

I wonder if strangers will sense our sorrow or our family's trespass. We walk beneath the CCTV's gaze, past the gumball machines and claw game, because this trip is compulsion: we needed a mission, a reason to leave my grandparents' sad house and drive, so we're here to buy something for our mom, a gift to express how sorry we are, her mother gone, her father in jail. It's absurd to think that anything from the self-checkout might bring comfort, but we fill a basket with herbal tea, a yellow flowering plant, women's magazines, and macadamia nuts. Grief makes you urgent and useless.

We did this a decade before, Mallory and I, in the wake of a different sadness during that Kentucky spring when our parents split up after twenty-four years. For that grief? We purchased candy-colored sundresses for our mom—fuchsia, yellow, electric blue—and pricy pink lipsticks from a makeup counter. As girls, we sensed what it meant to be a woman suddenly marriageless and stunned. Our other purchase? A gift certificate to our parents' favorite restaurant, the Spanish place on Bardstown Road, because we hoped like desperate kids in a bad family movie that this last-ditch date might make our parents remember their love. Instead, our dad moved into an apartment behind Bahama Breeze, I dropped my classes at the university midsemester, my brothers ghosted to their jobs and bands and girlfriends, and Mallory quit high school for an online GED program that we realized taught evangelical principles and dubious science as she sped through it to start college at sixteen. One morning, she, my mom, Cameron— my youngest brother—and I emptied the family house for a smaller split-level in La Grange, one with no history, the four of us rolling couches across the frosty front lawn and up the ramp of a moving truck because who can live on the set of a canceled television show? Only my oldest brother, Brendan, occupied the old family home until it sold, smoking weed and playing his Fender Strat in that museum of who we'd once been: the Christmases and movie nights and post-soccer spaghetti dinners while my mom's piano students' wobbly renditions of "Für Elise" echoed from the front room. We'd existed as that family for twenty-four years and now we were somehow over.

With the same adrenaline we'd used to haul coffee tables and holiday decorations to a new address, we siblings and our mom road-tripped to St. Augustine, Florida, where we walked along freezing, deserted beaches and sat on aluminum seats in a sea park to watch dolphins perform tricks for sardines and where we rented red scooters none of us were qualified to drive in traffic, arriving at the Fountain of Youth, which Ponce de León had bumped into when he claimed to discover Florida even though Florida was never lost, never needed discovering. And then we drove to New Orleans where we roamed the French Quarter and caught Bourbon Street beads flung from second-story balconies and drank hurricanes at Lafitte's until two a.m. because there weren't rules any longer, not even for my little sister. In the morning, we chased hangovers away with those boozy slushies that swirl in rainbow colors on every corner and that you carry out in plastic cups onto the ten a.m. street where tipsy others stumble toward tours of cemeteries or mansions. After that? Nashville, the Opryland Hotel. High above the lush ferns of the atrium I stood on the balcony in a complimentary bathrobe and watched a lone bird flap from tree to tree, lost inside the building forever.

In the aftermath: a road trip charged on a credit card, no sobriety or helmets, but room service French fries and hotel hot tubs instead while my mom quietly cried in the bathroom. Who were we now? I was twenty-three, the oldest kid. Old enough to know what, exactly, was ending. Old enough to think, *But we had been so happy*, and to wonder if it had all been a dream.

\/.

A week after the shooting, here he is, my grandfather, Bill, at home, bail posted, and there's nothing to do but wait for his fate, wait to see whether he'll face trial, whether he'll sit inside a prison cell for the rest of his life. His public defender issues rules for the interim: no guns in the house, no crossing state lines, and there are probably other things that Bill can't do, but I suspect he doesn't care because he's grieving his wife of sixty-three years, grieving the hospital plan that failed, the spring loosed from a cheap gun, and how, in that moment, on his knees on the linoleum, an officer running toward him, he knew he'd be arrested. Can anything possibly matter to a man after that? As I stand in his kitchen, I don't believe it can.

Bill's heart contains a sheep's valve from surgery one decade ago so, alongside the French roast my mother brews, she boils a pot of water for his caffeineless substitute of barley and ground chicory root and we three sit out on the front porch with ceramic mugs in our hands. Rabbits scrabble beneath the bird feeder, hawks dart above the pines, and it's so warm that I wear a sleeveless dress in January. He tells us that he slept like shit on the thin, suicide-watch mattress, but everyone was so kind and he read an entire novel in his cell, start to finish.

We pour refills inside, and that's when he gifts me Frances's wedding ring, places it in my palm and says, "I wish your grandma was here to give this to you instead." My mom jokes that she never would've done that, not Frances, that she would never have parted with her ring. We laugh at that truth. "No way!" Frances would've said while jerking her hand from me, joking like I'd try to steal it. "Fat chance!" But Frances told me one time on her back porch that I could have it, this keepsake from their 1950 elopement to Pioche, Nevada, the same ring that was stolen from their car when they swam at the beach as newlyweds. It somehow made its way to the LAPD and to her finger again—a second act, a sign of good luck.

I'd memorized this ring on her hand, and I'd also memorized Frances's hand, and the shape of her arm and, of course, her face and also her voice and I can hear the response she'd have to my grief. "Oh, Ash," she'd say, sad about my sadness, her tone almost admonishment. I replace the ring that's already on my finger, a different one that used to belong to Frances also, this costume jewelry piece with fake stones made from foil and glass set in real gold, a ring originally belonging to her neighbor Dottie in LA. And this fits, too, Frances's beautiful wedding ring, perfect on my finger, the intricate white gold setting with a modest diamond that, she used to say, sparkles, "really sings."

\/.

Later that night, Mallory sleeps a short drive away in her house with her two young sons. Cameron and his wife, Randie, sleep further out on a hilly, rural road, goats and chickens in their yard. Brendan sleeps in Texas, hanging on to some hard-won health and sobriety, working in hotel maintenance and watching bands play at night. I'm not sleeping: I'm staying with my mother and Earnhardt and my grandfather. The silence and darkness in a place where I normally feel at home could drown me: on high alert, I listen for sounds of drawers, doors, pill bottles, weapons, the car backing out of the garage. After all, the act my grandfather committed seems so incomprehensible that another dark thing must be coming. But the house stays silent except for the warm, familiar chimes of the grandfather clock.

The plant we bought my mom already droops. Even after a sleeping pill and hours of Netflix and FaceTiming Ryan, I'm restless in Frances's room. Could anything have stopped this? Did she take her own life by requesting it or did my grandfather take it without her asking? Mallory says she saw them whispering to each other at the hospital. Either way, it's what she wanted, what she said out loud. Stars crinkle the sky outside her window, the silhouette of the Sierras.

We won't have a funeral in the aftermath: our family doesn't do funerals, maybe because we're not religious, but still no one has ever explained this to me. After all, we like birthday parties with homemade cake and dance parties in the garage and summer potlucks where kids run around the lawn. But despite being people who say, "I love you," as we leave with aluminum-foiled leftovers only to call one another minutes later to say, "I'm home," maybe we're too practical for mourning rituals? I won't press this question and anyways: no funeral was Frances's wish. The best I'm left with is to walk onto her deck and try to conjure her. *Give me a sign,* I think. But nothing comes, not even a 1:26 a.m. half-breeze, and I'm stunned most of all by how she has become blank space, simply gone.

✔/◄

In the aftermath, my mom floats grocery store roses in the bathtub after a psychic says there's a curse on our family. The psychic makes this claim when my mom walks down Highway 395, walking just to cope, no destination, and enters the shop on a whim, a part-house, part-business, interrupting a conversation between a woman and a man who holds a baby in his arms. As the psychic begins her reading, my mom tells her nothing about our family, gives her zero. The curse is a first impression.

"I can tell you how to get rid of it," the psychic says. She examines my mother's palm, explains that a special spell will cost extra but my mom's money line reveals that this shouldn't be a problem. My mom agrees to it. The psychic instructs my mom to buy roses, place petals in the bathtub, and recite the words the psychic gives her. This stranger's instructions carry weight just like a page from the Eastern philosophy or self-help books my mom used to keep on her bathtub ledge, their pages dog-eared and warped with water. In our family's slack cosmology, signs exist anywhere you look for them: billboards and radio lyrics and the crinkled magazine in the doctor's office.

Beyond the shooting, other loss and suffering has just occurred in our family, other stories: Why *wouldn't* my mom buy the roses? If it takes a psychic's spell to mend us, so be it.

\/-

In the aftermath, our family pays new attention to language: we mentally note when a person says that the shooting *just blows them away* or how it's a *longshot* that Bill will avoid prison. It's strange how guns suddenly appear in ordinary phrases: *Under fire. Stick to your guns. Oh, shoot.* Sometimes we tease the sibling who said it, but we discover what we hadn't noticed before: that the language of guns is everyday American vocabulary.

"Remember when that happened?" we'll ask one another facetiously when it's just us together in backyard chairs or on the phone in our beds at night. It's another way of saying, *Oh, my god. Was that real?* as though the event has already drifted into family history like an unremarkable day we shared. And then there we go again, recounting the event in earnest, top to bottom, each from our separate vantage: *Were you in the shower or already in your car when you heard? Did Cameron call you first or did Mallory? What's the last thing you said to Frances? To Bill?*

We tether to one another in the aftermath, check in with extra calls and texts. I travel back home to Ryan, to my life of adjunct teaching in the fog above Los Angeles and among the palm trees of Orange County, but return to Nevada for long weekends. I want to settle within myself how to see this event because to read the news is to read the word *murder* attached to my grandparents' names when *murder* belongs on *Law & Order* reruns or in the old noirs Ryan reads—nowhere near our family. Plus, is it murder if someone wants to die? Surely there's a word for it? But this, too, is a quirk of language: *mercy killing* is closest, but what of my grandfather's attempt to take his own life, too? I jostle this around in my brain as I drive from campus to campus, park the truck, choke down half an apple, put on lipstick in the rearview mirror before I teach freshman English.

We startle easily: Mallory FaceTimes me one morning, her number lighting up my laptop as I type in bed and drink coffee. "I have something to tell you!" she says, joking at having popped up on my screen so suddenly, and even though it's an offhand, silly remark, I freeze at her words. She must see the fright on my face because she just as quickly says, "Oh, no! Kidding! I'm sorry!" But I'm vigilant in the aftermath. Anything is possible and I want to be prepared.

‸

My mother returns to the psychic's shop, post-roses, post–bathtub spell.

The psychic says it's not too late for the pricy, foolproof option, the one guaranteed to obliterate our family's bad luck: for a higher fee, the psychic will trek to San Francisco where she'll use her direct line to whoever's in charge to pray and chant for us. My mother, who has already forked over cash to this person in her grief and desperation, declines.

But before my mom leaves, she says to the psychic, "I have to tell you something: You know the man who shot his wife in the hospital and then tried to kill himself?"

Yes, the psychic does. It's a small enough town.

"Those are my folks," my mom says, offering confirmation that the woman might be psychic and not wrong about the curse thing.

‸

In the aftermath, politicians reach out about gun control agendas and right-to-die issues. They'd like to talk, but my mother is calling banks about bail money, settling my grandmother's matters, communicating with the public defender about what will happen to my grandfather.

In the aftermath, national news shows phone my family, but my family doesn't call back. One with doctors who discuss medical matters. Gossipy shows. Tabloid news. One reporter notes that "the person who answered the phone said they were too busy to talk."

Locally, my grandfather has appeared on the evening news so often in recent weeks that my mom wonders if he's identifiable to strangers in a vague "I've seen him before" way. She senses this at Katie's Country Kitchen when he goes with my mom and stepdad for an early dinner.

But there's empathy in the aftermath. Neighbors and friends say, "What an incredible love story!" "What an act of compassion." "They must have loved each other so much." One time just a few weeks later, a medical professional steps into an elevator with my mom and says, "You don't know me, but I know your family. And I understand why your dad did what he did."

In the aftermath, my grandfather's closest friend suggests that, if my grandfather does go to prison, maybe he can teach woodworking? I find this so incredibly tender and absurd, the idea that an old man will instruct joiner carpentry in a maximum security prison. I picture the tiny wooden figures he'd teach the other men to carve like the ones in the living room: a bear, a horse, a sailor in a heavy coat smoking a pipe.

In the aftermath, shootings in schools, in churches, in fields, in synagogues, in airports, at festivals.

In the aftermath, it's confirmed that my grandpa won't face the death penalty. My mom tells me this over the phone. The death penalty had never occurred to me and how does that phrase show up in a conversation about the man in her living room?

In the aftermath, someone asks our family to provide written statements to the public defender. I'm irrationally terrified that something I'll do or say will make me complicit, will get someone in trouble, will implicate our whole family. *Just tell the truth,* I think, knowing that there's more than one version, depending on how one might view my grandfather's actions.

I read everything I can about assisted suicide, something I'd never before considered but that suddenly seems pressing. I learn about countries that allow those with severe mental illness to legally end their psychological suffering. I read thoughtful essays by disability rights advocates who argue that legalizing death by choice puts vulnerable people at risk. I mull perspectives that examine the moral and legal and ethical implications of euthanasia. Everyone has a point, I think, as I sit in bed in Long Beach, not yet dressed, eating an avocado with a spoon as the sun slides across the sky, hours of my own life passing as I Google *right to die, right or wrong* and think about how Frances would tell me to get off the internet, get outside, life is short, have a little fun.

And besides, to the best of my knowledge: no existent policy could've helped Frances anyway because her condition wasn't terminal. What options do you have if you just don't want to be in pain any longer? Not many. But my mind returns to the proliferation of guns, our comfort with them, and the irony of right-to-die restrictions. In America, death is both sanctioned and against the rules.

↘╱◄

In the aftermath, my mom passes the psychic's shop once more. She looks through the window and sees that the house is dark and empty: there's no trace of the woman who would lift our family's bad luck, no man with a child in his arms. We'll never know where they went. Perhaps they headed toward the coast with prayers and petals for the living, for the dead—and after all this, how is it still a surprise that people can be here, standing in the front room of a house, existing inside their private lives, then simply vanish without an explanation?

LUCY, 1975

When Frances was in her fifties, she had surgery. My grandfather waited for her as the procedure became complicated and took hours longer than the doctors expected. She told me that, under anesthesia, she'd died. It was such a good feeling, she said, to revisit the happiest parts of her life, and that's when she saw her, her best friend, Lucy, who'd died years earlier from an illness.

"We didn't talk," my grandmother explained. "But she was wearing a green dress. And I kind of communicated to her, 'Alright, Lucy! You got your favorite color!'"

For that reason, Frances wasn't afraid of death and I have since then pictured heaven as a place not filled with cottonwoods but one where the women we love return to us, radiant and unabridged, burdenless, their destinies fulfilled. Where they finally find our faces and don't need to speak a word as they greet us in joy, in ease, in dresses sewn from fabric in the colors they loved most on earth.

SELECTED INTERNET
COMMENTS, 2014–2015

My husband is there on the third floor where the shooting took place, they aren't letting visitors in unless the patient you are visiting is critical . . . So can't see my husband today . . . Hope the woman pulls through that was shot, it isn't anything to joke about . . .

Reply

You need the whole story before making assumptions. Many family and all heartbroken. Please think of them and say prayers instead of jokes.

Reply

That is an awful place. My mom died there!!!!!!!

Reply

Maybe his Obamacare wasn't working and he thought NDOP could take care of his medical issues better

Reply

wow.. sucks..

Reply

The article says she was there for previous injuries . . . injuries from what or whom I wonder. Maybe he was a wife beater . . .
Reply

Was it mercy killing? Maybe wife was dying . . . it is sad. And my prayers go out to all of them.

Reply

Something is going on here. Carson City is a small town and strange things can happen in small towns. A couple of years ago there was a murder in a small town down the road from me. The DA cut a plea that was basically a slap on the wrist. There was outrage and the judge refused to accept the deal and the perp got 12 years. If the motion flies, it's likely the prosecution read the community right. The gun in the hospital is troubling even though it's a .22. Normally you'd do a plea bargain with probation (which would also set a bad precedent of sorts) I would guess but the family seems united and that may have been rejected.

Reply

If the motion flies, it's likely the prosecution read the community right.
Well, that says something about the community, and not something good.

Reply

Seems he could have used a more subtle method.

Reply

This situation is exactly while legal euthanasia needs to be available. It is a crime this poor man had to end his wife's life, and in the process ruin his own.

Reply

Tough call. At one time I was strongly opposed to euthanasia. But ... I've been diagnosed with a terminal illness, and now things are a bit different. I've lived in a 'palliative care facility' (we used to call these nursing homes) for almost seven months, and on the days I manage to roll around the facility (I'm wheelchair bound) I see people begging for death. Don't know what I'll do, but not going to judge anyone else.

Reply

A prosecutor's job is to 'seek justice.' A dismissal in this case is absolutely justice.

Reply

D.A.'s hate losing cases. That's why they're not going forward in this one.

Reply

murderer killed his wife like a sick dog

Reply

Good luck getting a conviction on that. Why don't you go ahead and try that case and waste the taxpayer dollars while you're at it.

Reply

I will pray for this man, his deceased wife and family.

Reply

Great legal precedent there. 'I didn't mean anything BAD by shooting him/her.'

Reply

This is exactly why I am for doctor assisted suicide. To force a spouse to take this kind of action is disgusting. To force someone who is suffering and does not want to continue on, to blow their brains out so other family members find them like that is barbaric. For those so opposed to it, get off the religion kick and show some humanity.

Reply

It is always evil, gravely so, to purposely take the life of an innocent human being from the moment of conception until natural death.

He should be put on trial.

Reply

The DA should be fired. It's up to the judge or the jury to find him not guilty or the governor to pardon or commute his sentence.

Reply

A man who answered the phone at Dresser's home declined comment to the *Daily News* on Monday.

Reply

TRANSCRIPT: CELEBRITIES

ASHLEY FARMER: Where were you playing hooky?

FRANCES DRESSER: Downtown Broadway, at one of the shows. They came with a flashlight: "Let me see your identification." And the movie was *Where Are Your Children?* [*Laughs.*]

AF: Would you get in trouble for skipping?

FD: Ditching? Yeah.

AF: What high school did you go to?

FD: Franklin.

AF: And what were some of the places you would go to in town? Like if you'd get on the streetcar you'd go to the beach.

FD: And I'd have to transfer to the red car to get to the beach.

BILL DRESSER: The only buses you'd see back then were the Greyhound buses. Everything else was streetcars.

FD: They shouldn't have ever taken them out. That's not just my idea: I've even read it. The rubber companies—

BD: And the batteries.

FD: And the batteries.

BD: Willard. They wanted buses where they could sell more tires and more batteries.

FD: The good old days when the best we had was very bad [*laughs*].

AF: Did you ever see any famous people or do you remember any stories from those times?

BD: I saw George Raft.

FD: I saw that guy who smoked in advertisements for Philip Morris.

BD: I saw him, too, when I was in the service in New York.

FD: I didn't see very many celebrities.

BD: We used to see them in Santa Monica there—I used to hang around there quite a bit. And I saw the guy who played Dagwood, Arthur Lake. He used to play Dagwood in the movies and he had a yacht down there. I saw Errol Flynn. He had a yacht down there in Santa Monica. I'm trying to think of the name of his yacht.

FD: Boy, that Errol Flynn. Did you ever see a picture of him?

AF: Mm-hmm.

FD: Whew. When we were young, we really thought he was hot.

AF: Did you ever see them filming things?

FD: You could see them filming up there in those hills. I was over at my mom's. Della [FD's sister] and I were going to go somewhere— we were going to go to Highland Park—and she says, "Oh, we can't go there: they're filming a film up there and it'll be hectic."

I saw Judy Garland.

AF: You did?

FD: Yeah.

AF: Where?

FD: Easter sunrise services.

AF: Really? You just saw her? She was just ... in the congregation?

FD: No, she sang.

AF: That's neat. Was it a big deal that you saw her at the time?

FD: Big deal.

AF: What about musicians? Are there other people you saw perform?

FD: Oh, yeah. Because they used to have a performance down at the Million Dollar Theater in between the movies. I saw Gene Krupa.

BD: Drummer.

FD: He was a famous drummer back then. And Eddie Peabody, the banjo player. I saw him.

BD: I never went to very many movies. I remember I went to the Carthay Circle and watched *Snow White and the Seven Dwarfs*.

FD: Yeah, we saw that, too.

BD: I was pretty young at the time. My sister and I got on the streetcar and went there.

FD: What was that singer who was popular? "Hey now, just because my hair is curly. Just because my teeth are pearly?" Oh, he was popular then. I can't think of his name.

I know people who weren't from there used to think you'd see movie stars walking up and down the street.

AF: Did you ever think it was a big deal that you lived in California?

FD: No.

BD: Uh-uh.

Venice Pier was a pretty good pier back then. And there'd be a lot of people—rich people—that would go there and get on this taxi and take it out to the gambling barges—they had to be outside the three-mile limit. And people'd go down just to watch some celebrities get on the water taxis and go out there.

FD: It was really cool for us to see Judy Garland and see her sing in person because we just thought she was *it*.

AF: Was this after she'd done any big things?

FD: We knew who she was, so she must've been in some stuff.

AF: You were at church?

FD: No, Easter sunrise services. I don't know where we used to go—I think up at Forest Lawn—and she sang there. Jo [FD's sister] and I really liked Judy Garland.

BD: This was after I got out of the service, maybe 1948. I was in Trocadero and the orchestrator was the one who was married to Lucille Ball, Desi Arnaz.

In the casino, they had some bars where you could get a drink or beer. And they had, like, two bands. They'd alternate. Well, I was just sitting there talking to this guy and it was Desi Arnaz. And I didn't realize it and didn't think anything of it. We were just having a general conversation and later I looked up there and there he was leading his band [*laughs*].

FD: "What the hell's he doing up there?" [*Laughs*].

BD: Yeah, it was quite a coincidence.

AF: Did you recognize him after?

BD: I recognized when he replaced the other band. He was just taking a break and getting a drink. And the bar was a small one. They had a bigger one there, but this was the small one, and I was just sitting there and it was him and myself and maybe another couple of people. Talking, you know. And I hadn't paid much attention to the orchestra or anything.

CONTRADICTION, 2014

That compassion can also be a crime. That Frances never wanted a funeral or commotion when she died, but that her death and its details appeared on the television news, in print, discussed by strangers. That my grandfather is the steady one and that this same rationality compels him to commit an act that's beyond comprehension. That modern medicine can offer you more life than you want but no exit. That the day Bill shoots her in the hospital is one of my family's worst and yet it also offers relief. That as much as I wish my grandfather hadn't done what he did, I don't know if I would undo it.

TWO

AMERICAN DREAM JOB

I ease our ancient Isuzu Hombre up the Pacific Coast Highway, speeding above the sparkling coast and Donald Trump's shuttered cliffside golf course where the eighteenth hole has slid into the sea. It's 2012. Work-bound and buoyed to teach, I'm headed to the campus that a fellow adjunct described as "pricy and relaxed like a drug rehabilitation center." I've only taught at this school for eight weeks, but my view differs: these students seem motivated and earnest. They're studying to become physical therapists and filmmakers and public defenders and environmentalists. During our fairy tale unit, they argue that the Disney princesses are actually feminists. They dodge curse words when we read aloud. They don't smoke after class. A less cynical generation than mine, they believe that the world can improve even though, in their eyes, it's not half bad.

This spirit is infectious: a dangerous adjunct optimism flutters inside me. I'm convinced that as long as I'm positive and grateful and hardworking—grinding forward, teaching beyond reproach, proving myself a team player—one of the three places where I work will hire me full time. *We'll even keep this shitty truck with its busted A/C,* I think. See, bargaining is a Kübler-Ross stage of grief, even though I still sense the life I want with its attendant stability and living wage just inches beyond my reach.

I park the pickup in the school lot filled with students' Mercedes Benzes and BMWs and that one baby-blue Bentley while hoping no one spots me hauling essays from this ride that people have twice left notes on with offers to buy for cash. I'm embarrassed to be driving this, I realize, peeling my sweaty body from the hot bench seat, and then I'm embarrassed to be embarrassed about something so superficial as a car, as money.

The following semester, at another college where I teach writing in the evenings, we discuss *Fear and Loathing in Las Vegas* and Hunter S. Thompson's account of the vapid, violent mangling of the American Dream. The theme of our writing class is the counterculture of the 1960s. We read about the civil rights movement and women's liberation and Vietnam War protests. I ask the students if counterculture exists today and, if so, what is it countering? I'm jotting their list on the whiteboard when a quiet student's outburst startles the room. "This shit matters!" he says almost by accident, unfiltered, the words leaving his lips as it occurs to him. I agree. We talk about how reading and writing can change things.

And while I believe the words that leave my own mouth, I wouldn't blame students for calling me a hypocrite. Because the truth is that, while I do trust that reading and writing can change things, in that moment I know I need to change my own life at thirty-three, one in which I'm barely making it, have zero security from one month to the next, zero benefits, zero prospects. Plus, if I participate in this system designed to make education a more lucrative business, aren't I complicit? As I stand at the board, sun setting beneath the classroom shades, I wonder if it's wrong to imply that if students work hard in this class, reading and writing and thinking—if they work hard in school, period—that it'll add up to something.

✓⌐

Still: it often feels like a sweet dream, the challenging conversations about books, the students so intense and numerous and vivid, their essay arguments, their multiple revisions, their lives textured with fellowships and babies and court dates and requests for letters of recommendation, all of this filling my inbox and office hours and online class portal before the semester ends when, poof, they vanish, the serious students and the jokesters and the overachievers. Each semester equals a chapter of crazed survival, of stacks of students' words on my coffee table, of miniscule-yet-vivid details from my commutes like the Los Angeles billboards advertising new seasons of old television procedurals and the alien, fragile flowers along the coast that shoot toward a daytime moon and the scent of musk sage mixed with sea air as I drive with the windows down.

In *Fear and Loathing in Las Vegas*, the protagonist Raoul Duke rents red, then white, American-made convertibles to tool around Vegas in as he probes the rotten heart of our country. Students write essays about the decadent cars, analyzing the colors and what it means for Thompson's alter ego to pursue his journalistic mission in style as the cars get trashed. Conversations require historical context—LSD, footage from Altamont, microlessons on Richard Nixon and Muhammad Ali. Yet, despite the briefcases full of drugs that don't quite resonate and the satire that sometimes falls flat, most students seem to find a connection to their own experiences as young people in this country.

One evening, I ask students whether or not there's such a thing as the American Dream. The question hangs beneath the classroom lights. A few of the students look at me like I'm ridiculous. Their faces ask, *Why else would I work two jobs to go to school? Why would I sacrifice so much? Why would I even be here?*

✦✦✦

In Syracuse, where I was privileged to attend graduate school on a creative writing fellowship after a couple of failed tries, I leaned against a friend's shoulder in one of our drafty, rented Victorian apartments as we sipped beer with others on election night and waited to see if Barack Obama would become our next president. We sucked a collective breath, gripped one another's forearms and shoulders as we waited for the official announcement. What luck that we'd found one another, that we could study writing at a time when our country was on the cusp of promise. We were, most of us, intoxicated and hopeful and broke, optimistic about our country, youngish but not so young as to not understand the significance of this moment, all of us tipsy and cheering.

For me, it was a powerful era of firsts: living solo in my own studio apartment after an early marriage and divorce, writing with discipline, taking classes in vine-covered brick buildings like I'd only seen in movies, living on the opposite side of the country, far from my family, and finding kinship with other writers. Then came teaching: two weeks in, I thought, *This is what I want to do with my life*, an idea that crystallized as I talked with eighteen-year-olds about bell hooks, jittery and energized, nervous that I'd fumble difficult discussions but hopeful that a Gen Ed requirement many students loathed could be halfway meaningful. Even the minutiae of drafting assignments and grading responses in a coffee shop while snow piled up beneath the streetlights excited me. I'd found my path. It would be competitive, sure—our professors made no bones—but I figured I could throw my heart into it while being tenacious. I wouldn't be picky about where I taught, what schools or workloads or course types. It wouldn't matter as long as I got to do this. And I knew I could work hard: I'd had stints of jug-gling multiple jobs before, logging long hours and finding time to write, staying late at businesses where I was a receptionist or an administrative assistant and the bosses were kind enough to let me linger after hours to work on my own stuff as the nighttime lights of Santa Monica or Louisville flipped on and twinkled.

Approaching thirty, after a string of random gigs and failures and cross-country moves motivated by half-cooked plans, I'd felt certain about what I wanted—finally, suddenly, in a burst of idealism like a bomb. Another first.

◆╱◄

My favorite storytellers were Frances and Bill, who had a captive audience in me, their eldest grandchild, who loved imagining 1930s Los Angeles, the ocean and orange groves, the sound of Tommy Dorsey's big band or the generous movie producer who lived near Frances's family and stopped by to give them gifts because he knew money was always tight for them. How Frances shared a bed with her sisters, several of them crowded together, and how Bill's family absconded from rent collectors by switching addresses across the South Bay. How Frances pressed vinyl at Capitol Records, quitting high school without telling her parents, sneaking her dad's white shirts and drawing a stocking line up the back of her leg with an eyebrow pencil. How Bill enlisted in the Navy at seventeen. Their photos from this era glow like Hollywood movie stills: Frances in a lacy slip at the edge of a desert lake as my shirtless grandfather kisses her. Or the two of them dressed up, him in pressed slacks, her in a dress with a heart-shaped neckline as she perches on the edge of his car.

Then their story shifts: Frances gets pregnant, Bill lands a job at the Long Beach shipyard. Once they had a baby, that's when the party ended, Frances joked. They bought a small home. They took camping vacations, tinseled their Christmas tree with presents beneath it, wore matching family pajamas for a holiday photo. Why did this feel nostalgic to me, these stories I'd recorded on tape, then cell phone, as I sat with Bill and Frances in their living room over the years, me the kid who wanted to keep them alive forever, but also sought instruction from them on how to live a happy, useful life?

It's privilege that lets me feel any fondness for earlier eras, and the American Dream has never been equal opportunity. But my grandparents' stories reinforced the myth that if you chose a path and worked hard you could expect to do as well, at least, as your parents had. Their stories made it feel linear, uncluttered: if you built boats, you were a boat builder. If you taught, you were a teacher. Pick a road and try your best. As I rush between campuses, I sense my pathlessness, the red truck drifting from lane to lane, non-job to non-job, and I figure maybe I want too much.

Write down three things that you're glad for each day, the gratitude app on my phone instructs. From a parking lot I write *my heart, my mom, Ryan, my students, food to eat, books, trees* which is twice as many as it asks you to log each day.

᛭

One night, I dream about a woman I don't recognize. We're at a noisy holiday party and she approaches me to chat. She tells me she's an adjunct instructor. She's ready to explain what an adjunct is but I wave my hands like, *Oh, I already know—you don't have to tell me.*

"No," she yells over the noise. "You don't understand."

She explains that, yes, she's an adjunct instructor. But she's also an adjunct friend, adjunct wife, adjunct mother, adjunct family member. She's an adjunct in everything she does. She lists them on her fingers, counting four, five, six, seven.

"I never know when they're going to need me," she says, her face full of despair. I hate this party and want to call it a night. Her existence is one big contingent gig.

◂╱◂

In counterculture class, we read a piece about the *homo sacer*. To put it simply: The homo sacer is the idea of a person who lives on the fringe of society. The law defines him as an outsider but, because of that, he's also outside the law's protection. The homo sacer can be killed and the killer won't receive punishment—the homo sacer is on his own, outside anyone's jurisdiction. In the essay we read, the author applies this idea to Raoul Duke and Dr. Gonzo as they gobble drugs and observe society from its crumbling edge. After class, I hold office hours on a picnic table in the quad while, in nearby buildings, administrators I've never met determine whether I'll keep teaching or not. And when one of my classes gets cut days before the next semester begins—thereby denting my income in frightening ways—there's no protection, no one to follow up with, no identifiable person at the other end of that decision.

◂╱◂

Students test how personal they can get with me, their professor-who's-not-a-professor: when I mention that I jog, they ask how far, where. I refer to "my partner" and students ask who it is, what they do for a living. "Where did you get those cute boots?" a freshman asks. "Can I friend you on Facebook?" a guy close to my age jokes,

49

teasing in a friendly way. I keep my professional distance, but there's also a secondary impulse to protect students from the truth about my tenuous employment, my weird status, the fact that I'm not really an employee-employee, just a person who showed up to campus ten minutes ago to make half the pay of a faculty member.

And then there's the student each semester who lingers after class and says, "I want to do what you do for a living." They'll ask how I got into teaching, what classes I took, what I studied in graduate school. I answer honestly but I never endorse this path—I toe the line of careful, vague encouragement. When the same student asks what I'm teaching next semester because they want to take another class with me, I admit that I don't know if I'll be back. I can't be candid and say that I'm considering quitting, that I've been doing middle-of-the-night research on radiology tech programs and fantasizing about wearing a tropical shirt at Trader Joe's because I'd have dental and get discounted groceries and work with people whose names I'd know—people who seem happy. I don't mention that I made better money years ago without this terminal degree, back when, as a receptionist, I wrote stories and read celebrity gossip online and answered ten brief phone calls across an entire workday.

But here's a truth: the only time I'm truly present—not anxiously weighing whether I chose the wrong course and how to correct it—is, ironically, when I'm teaching in front of the whiteboard or meeting students for one-on-one conferences. That's when I'm in, all in, unable to fret or project beyond the end of the class. The only thing that keeps me from worrying about the path I'm on is being on it.

✓

At one of the schools, graduation day arrives. The department requests staff volunteers to help. It's a Saturday when I should be grading students' final portfolios, but I add my name to the list. I know by now there's no proving myself, but it'll feel sweet to cheer on some of the graduates, so I dress up, drive to Los Angeles from Long Beach, feeling the sun's rays through my window. When I arrive on campus, my name isn't on the volunteer list. "You can hand out programs," the coordinator says, even though there are too many people already doing this, competing to give them to the guests who trickle into the tent. The day glimmers, palm trees swaying, students giddy with their proud parents who hold on to wiggly younger siblings. I have no reason to be here, I realize, so somewhere around the H names, I get in the car and leave.

∿

If I sense the homo sacer within me—if I suspect that I could be nixed because of my outsider status—the fear manifests on a crystalline first day of the spring semester at one of the schools where I teach. What happens is this: an administrator walks along our row of classrooms, popping his head through open doors to say hello, and then he enters mine as I'm ready to take attendance. He turns his back to the room so that he faces only me, mouths an off-color comment, then leaves.

As I drive to my next class, the strange moment rattles me even though I don't know what to make of it, or him, a person I've only talked to a few times in what have been brief, if awkward, con-versations. When he requests a meeting in his office the following week, I figure he wants to clear things up and apologize. Instead, the meeting becomes about my teaching, something he has never seen. He suggests that students could be taking my classes because I must not grade hard enough, that they communicate these things to one another via secret networks. This, despite never having been questioned about my grades these past four years. Despite my always having that range, As to Fs, each semester. Despite there being no stated expectations or even norming sessions besides the sample essay response I was required to complete when I interviewed for the position. *So here it is,* I think, *the shoe dropping,* and it feels like being crushed, sitting in the administrator's leather chair between bookshelves, sunlight streaming onto the floor and my feet.

I don't escape either when, a few weeks later, a tenured colleague I've never met comes to sit in on my class one soggy afternoon. It's a planned, routine thing—other adjuncts are being observed, too. Our class is analyzing Adrienne Rich's poem "Diving into the Wreck" and as I pass out materials to small groups, he hovers near me, waxing conspiratorially about how he'd rather be somewhere else just listening to the sound of the rain rather than doing this observation. Later, as we wait outside the door beneath the eaves for students to write feedback about me, he explains how he didn't really want to be a professor at this school, didn't want this job at all, how he had other, more lucrative offers for positions at other schools, and this place—the school I've long fantasized about teaching at as a legitimate hire one day—coaxed him into the gig. He shrugs his shoulders and sighs like, *Eh, it's good enough, I guess.* He tells me my lesson was excellent. He says it's exactly how he would've done it.

The students leave. I gather up my whiteboard pens and the scattered leftover copies of poems, ready to commute to my next school. But my colleague stops me: "I've been instructed to talk to you about your trouble grading." He tells me I need to set up times to meet with him throughout the rest of the semester.

Take me out of it, a privileged white woman raised by boomers who reinforced the idea that I could achieve if I worked hard enough: I understand that I'm not so special, despite what my unearned advantages told me. Plus, I picked a competitive field and knew any steady college teaching gig would be tough to get. And yet, it's not mutually exclusive of the fact that there is a deep problem within this system.

While I'd like to claim that adjunctification will hurt American higher education, I'm not sure that's the case: higher ed seems to work just fine. Students encounter competent, passionate instructors who toil in the system despite all that's rotten—and usually because the instructors love teaching. In fact, students are likely to take classes with gunners and idealists who throw themselves into it, trying to prove their worth while knowing that this might be as good as it gets. Docile and sometimes ashamed, unable to be "difficult" or make demands, some of us won't even divulge our tenuous status to our students. Academic departments thrive with a stable of instructors at the ready; additional course sections can be added a day or two before the start of the semester and someone hungry—figuratively, maybe literally—will snap them up. It's a lucrative business model, the supply of instructors willing to work for pennies and without benefits outweighing the demand. So what's the cost?

It's near the end of the book when Raoul Duke says to

someone decades his junior, "Just be thankful your heart is young and strong." I quit those schools soon after that rainy observation. I still think about that student and his exclamation about what matters, still wonder about so many students who, by now, are teachers and doctors and artists and parents in this world, one in which the man who owned the defunct golf course is now our president, a time in which we distrust facts and degrade education and need the sharpest critical thinking skills while impeachment hearings fill our screens. If adjunct teaching creates damage, it's a soft harm that's often imperceptible. The kind of failure we might think and read and write about, even when we're not so young and our hearts aren't quite as strong.

SLOW CIRCLES

[*The moon pulls the ocean. The sun assists. We find comfort in these facts, even if we're adrift. Even if we see that we're small, brief people on an also-small planet, treading water in an ocean of stars.*]

Years before I marry Ryan, we slow dance at my first wedding.

The deejay cues Eric Clapton's "Wonderful Tonight," a song from the wrong era, wrong even back when it was my glittery high school prom theme. Those first few notes of slide guitar: identifiable to every guest in this Seelbach Hotel ballroom. Lights dim. Where has the groom gone? A friend notes the awkwardness of a bride standing solo on the dance floor, so she shoves Ryan, the nearest uncoupled man, in my direction. We've met a few times. He's my brother Brendan's guest and I know him from his visits to the Speed Avenue apartment my sibling and I recently shared.

Ryan places his hands on my waist and we sway in the lights. I ask where his longtime girlfriend is. "We broke up," he says and I tell him I'm sorry to hear it. We went to a concert once—he and his girlfriend, my brother, the groom and I, all of us squeezed in a tight row at the Palace while Wilco played on a blue-lit stage. Dancing with Ryan now on my wedding day, I'm conscious of my body's closeness to someone I don't know well, of the slow circles our feet make, of the overwhelm of this evening, people I love from each era of my life either turning on the dance floor or drinking at tables dotted with tea lights and rose petals.

We talk about Los Angeles, how I'm moving there in a month.

He says he's been a few times on road trips with friends. He likes it out west.

Then the song ends, the colorful lights spin, the reception becomes a party again, and the groom returns to my side as guests celebrate until the crowd thins to those like my brothers and Ryan and the groom, too, who filter to the downstairs bar of this place that F. Scott Fitzgerald wrote about in *The Great Gatsby*. I take the brass elevator alone to my suite to ditch my dress for a robe and pull pins from my hair in the bathroom where wrapped soaps sit in a crystal dish against the mirror. In bed, I read cards from family and friends. July fifth. "Congratulations on your first wedding!" Brendan had teased me earlier that night as we clinked drinks.

A month later, I move to Santa Monica, California. I'll begin, then drop out of, graduate school at USC for professional writing, while the groom attends Playhouse West Acting School. We find day jobs and an apartment ten blocks from the beach, a nondescript one-bedroom we can afford because it sits above a paint store parking lot where delivery trucks beep all day, sunrise to sunset, incessant. Still, if I tiptoe high on the bathtub's edge at the correct angle, there it is, the shimmer of sea—a blue crescent no bigger than my thumbnail.

In the mostly empty apartment, I write post-wedding thank-you notes. I send Ryan one for his present: a monetary gift and card with happy wishes, written in his scribble that I know so well now. In my note to him, I mention the Pacific. I describe the Ferris wheel at the pier because it feels like a convincing, joyful detail—never mind that I've never ridden it, only watched it spin from the shore, turning like a bright clock.

A few months later, Ryan sends a thank-you for our thank-you note. *Who does that?* I think. He tells me I was a lovely bride and that the groom was handsome, too. "I hope California is everything you expected it to be. After all, it's the end of the line," he writes. He quotes David Berman, a Nashville poet and musician who often kicks around Louisville: "And somehow the ocean is always there to make us feel stupid." November twelfth, 2003.

Palm trees sway, green and gold. I answer phones at a financial think tank's front desk on Ocean Avenue where waves roll outside the window twelve to twenty-four times per minute, hundreds of times per hour, thousands per day, an endless glimmering loop. The ocean does, indeed, make me feel stupid. Ryan and I aren't in touch again for years.

[*The ocean isn't actually blue: that's a trick of light. The ocean is only blue the same way that seashells make the sound of crashing waves. Even children understand these illusions, and yet we wouldn't paint the sea—wouldn't even daydream it—any other way.*]

I wasn't always a bride, didn't always want to be her. I fell head-first for others without wanting forever, like the photographer I nearly lived with for a blissed-out year before we hugged goodbye and returned our books and hoodies and stacks of photographs to each other in the movie theater parking lot. Or the guy a decade older than me who left paperbacks against my torn screen door before disappearing through the Back Door for too many drinks too late at night, a person with secrets, I suspected, but didn't mind. And there was the woman who said, "We can't just run off together" as we sat on her floor, legs crossed, facing each other while the pink sun crashed behind the snowy horizon and my heart quivered. For stretches, I couldn't care less about rings and veils. Other times, I relished being all by myself.

Yet, in those bright spring months before I get engaged, I'm convinced that what I need is a direct path, a clear shot. Toward what? I couldn't say. But I'm sick of spinning in place and believe in some unconscious way that marriage might mean a straight line or way forward. I feel this so fervently that a late summer day at the county pool with the not-yet-groom transforms from lazy sunbathing in plastic lounges near the deep end into something serious. By the time we drive home in the Kentucky dusk, windows down, sunburned and certain enough in each other as the hills roll by, I have plans to marry the guy I went to prom with several years ago.

✦

[*There's a spot in the ocean so remote that, if a person stood there, they'd be closer to outer space than to anyone else on Earth. In other words, it's possible to be so far from land and the people you love that the stars in the sky are a better bet for companionship.*]

Unhappiness isn't a word on my lips. I'm determined to make this new life of mine fit, to stick it out. But I'm lost in Los Angeles, both metaphorically and literally: as I drive home late at night after class, I regularly get turned around in the dark, confused on interstates that look identical and loop around one another, the whole time feeling bone-certain that the wrong direction is actually correct. One time, I drive for forty minutes only to end up behind the building I just left. I call the groom from my car so he can help me navigate. "Which exit do you see?" he asks, but the number is meaningless.

When Brendan calls from Kentucky and we catch up about

television and music and his new girlfriend, I don't breathe a word of discontent. Still, he teases me once, apropos of nothing, "You should've married Ryan Ridge."

Around the time I get married, Ryan logs a lot of hours in Louisville dives and Nashville honky-tonks. David Berman does the same. If Ryan visits Nashville, he and his cousin might say, "Let's find Berman," and go to the Gold Rush knowing they'll run into him. Over the years, Ryan and Berman collide like that, sometimes in states of disrepair, and once for a parking lot snowball fight with other friends. At Seidenfaden's, an old Louisville bar, they talk over gin and tonics about Berman's poem "The High Numbers," which was just published in *The Believer*. Berman says he has a better poem, "About the Party," coming out with them soon.

"Ryan," he says before leaving, "I just want my poetry to get you laid."

"I don't know if you write that kind of poetry," Ryan says.

◣╱◢

[*The longest a person has been lost at sea and survived? 438 days. He kept track of time by watching the phases of the moon. He actively day-dreamed—delicious meals, sex, long walks outdoors—so vividly that, even when he found land and recovered, those hallucinations remained tangible like memories from life. His imagination, it seems, sustained him.*]

When Ryan learns from Brendan that I'm separated and living in Nevada near my family, he sends me an email with the subject: "Steroid Prayers." He says he's sorry to hear about the breakup. Toward the end of the brief note, he suggests that the two of us exchange writing sometime. Eventually we do. We attach poems and stories to emails that become longer over months that pass, messages in which we make up absurd questionnaires for each other and relay minute details from our days. "My writing desk is a broken ping-pong table piled high with reference books, rock CDs, a bag of cheap grass, and a Dell laptop," he writes. He tells me about the classes he's taking, his final semester after five different undergrad schools, including film school in Pittsburgh and our local community college and the same hometown university that Cameron, Mallory, and I all went to. He sends me jokes he's writing, one-liners because stand-up is his backup plan even though it's not clear what his primary plan might be. It's not like I have plans either: I tell him about coaching gymnastics in the desert while living with my mom—a life I couldn't have predicted when we'd danced together a few years back.

We bond over James Tate, Denis Johnson. We commiserate about winter feeling extra icy, extra long. He sends me the poem Berman had told him about, the poem about a party, likely set in Louisville, where the speaker sees a woman and her boyfriend. In it, he notices her ears, "the two beautiful pink wheels they are." He refers to a downtown fair that I know well, one that happens every year. "I thought I'd send it along because it reminded me of you for some odd reason," Ryan writes. We start talking on the phone after work, after evenings out with friends, all night sometimes, me whispering from my mom's living room couch or the guest bed, him always staying up later than me, three time zones in the future.

I visit for one week that spring. I'm twenty-eight. We read Berman's poem "Self-Portrait at 28," out loud when we're tipsy on bench seats that live in the basement near the ping-pong table, a driver's and passenger's side extracted from someone's car, the seat belt hardware still attached. It's a long poem, one that winds and circles, returns to itself. It's written, it seems, for people just a little older than us in the post-9/11 George Bush years—the true Gen Xers, though we're just enough on the cusp to relate to aspects of it, like anticipating watching the world end from a beautiful hill. Reading a poem out loud with another person is something I haven't done as an adult. It's not unlike slow dancing.

When he leaves for work, I'm asleep in his bed. "I drove away and left you sleeping in my bed," Ryan emails me that same day because email is still how we know each other best. He sends me a poem he heard that morning on the radio. In it, two strangers in a pawn shop look at one of those illusion paintings made from ink blots, the kind that Freud used. The shopkeeper says that a person sees either an image of lovers or a picture of a skull. If it's the latter, he says, that person is all but doomed.

The strangers both see skulls. "And have been together ever since," it ends.

〳⁄ˍ

[*More than half of the oxygen we breathe comes from the sea. No matter where we are or who we're with, we might remember that the ocean keeps us alive.*]

Months later, I sit on a barstool in the bachelors' Baringer Avenue kitchen. I'd moved back to Louisville just the day before: with my inner compass still busted, I knew to return to the city I belong to more than any other, to my friends and some of my family, to roads I know by heart, to a place where I might find a better job than coaching. Plus, there's Ryan now, Ryan who pours us drugstore mimosas to celebrate my return to town. We hug, toast. He tops us off and bubbles go to our heads. We kiss.

Then his sister bursts through the door with a sob. Their

grandmother, Margie, has died. Margie, who smoked Pall Mall non-filters like Vonnegut and had busted Ryan out of preschool for ice cream trips. Margie, who admonished him to get haircuts and still slipped him occasional fun money. Who lived just down the road and helped raise him.

I sober up, say goodbye. Ryan spends the next day typing her eulogy on the ping-pong table. When I meet his mother for the first time, it's before she leaves for the funeral home.

And that's how our life together starts: a beginning threaded with endings.

Ryan works as a medical courier, ferrying organ coolers and high-priced joint replacement parts to hospitals across the tristate. I answer phones in a downtown Louisville high-rise filled with lawyers, accountants, tax professionals: if something breaks, they call my desk and I, in turn, call the maintenance team who'll fix it. Once per month, I hand out coffee and Krispy Kreme donuts in the lobby to every tenant who spills through the heavy glass doors. My job is nearly unnecessary: I'm a friendly go-between. But I'm grateful for employment and when I fret about where I'm headed, Ryan reminds me that this gig is temporary, encourages me to have fun, to keep writing. He doesn't worry. When I call him at lunch from the courtyard fountain, he answers by either turning down the radio from the road or waking up from a park near the Ohio where he's napping between long drives.

We give up sleep: at night we hang out in his tidy, book-filled bedroom in the Baringer Avenue house at the edge of Cherokee Park or on the wide front porch with his roommates or with our friends at Highlands dives or with Brendan sometimes or at the apartment I move into with my best friend, Katie, a place with sage-green walls and lopsided floors near breweries that people stumble out of at four a.m., sometimes hooting or singing as they spill across our lawn.

Ryan and I spend our extra seconds with each other, but when we're apart, we write emails or burn elaborate mix-CDs with collaged, homemade covers: Pavement, Elvis, the Pixies, the Modern Lovers. As we talk, we uncover every place our lives converged in Louisville without us knowing it, every time our circles overlapped—the rock shows and readings and events, like the time Hunter S. Thompson came for keys to the city, something I'd helped organize as a freshman from my dorm room: Ryan had sat in the audience while Warren Zevon played onstage and I'd watched from behind heavy velvet curtains. Or years later, the Fourth of July party where Ryan had stood with his girlfriend in the same crowded house I'd shown up at with a group of friends and the not-yet-groom.

"You had on a white belt," Ryan remembers. "He was standing behind you, a little PDA. You appeared happy."

✓⁄◄

[Do you know that there are enormous lakes and miles-long rivers inside the ocean—bodies of water inside larger bodies of water? Do you know about the deep-down mountain range that covers more than 31,000 miles? How about the blue whales with hearts the size of Hondas? The pressure so intense at the deepest points of the sea that it'll make our man-made equipment implode? How you can sit at an Ocean Avenue reception desk, watching the water for hours without knowing how much you don't know?]

"If I'm going to do it at all, I have to do it now or I never will," Ryan says about applying to graduate school for creative writing.

I've been back in Louisville for a few months, and it wasn't long ago that I'd abandoned the night program in Los Angeles that I couldn't afford and the marriage I couldn't make stick. *Well, I think, if he's going to leave, I can't just stay here, passing out donuts in my dress shoes.* I decide to apply to writing programs, too, but this time only to dream schools with bad odds and good funding.

After work, I stop rushing to meet him at Baringer when the clock strikes five: I stay behind, the last one in the office. I open a Word doc and work on the same twelve poems after my boss dims the fluorescent lights and the bright disk of a sun slips down to make way for the moon.

"We'll get into the same program," Ryan says and, though that math looks bad, I somehow believe him.

We don't get into the same program.

Instead, we'll spend three years nearly as far apart from each other as possible: I'll head to upstate New York and he'll go to Southern California, the place I recently left, a fifteen-minute drive to the coast, 2,675 miles between us.

Our second year of grad school, we travel home to Louisville for the holiday break. I drive my Honda, now rusted at the bottom from road salt, eleven hours through the Syracuse snow, then Buffalo snow, then Pennsylvania's and Ohio's, stopping once to catnap at a gas station like Ryan used to in his courier days. He flies from Irvine with a light coat, a Californian now. We'll stay with family for three weeks except for one night at a downtown hotel, a minivacation within our vacation—a stay at the Seelbach, the spot where I married years ago.

We check in to our room, then drink a bourbon in the dim downstairs piano bar. We explore the hotel's long hallways, the basement room with zodiac signs embossed in gold across the leather ceiling, and the ballroom where my wedding reception took place—where he and I had danced as acquaintances several years before. The ballroom is dark but unlocked. We walk across the parquet floor to the window overlooking downtown and its twinkling lights. I'm standing in my past, present, and future. In the morning, I'm in a hotel robe when he asks me to marry him.

✧

[*There are 20 million tons of gold floating in the ocean.*]

We've been engaged for years, have long lived in California, have ridden the Santa Monica Ferris wheel together, have shared an apartment and bills, sickness and health, family births and deaths and changes, all by the time we actually decide to make it legal for practical reasons. We briefly consider a backyard desert party in Bill and Frances's yard, but the logistics are tricky. "And besides," Ryan says, "I was at your first wedding"—that's close enough for him, good enough for me.

Instead, we marry that November at a kind writer-friend's home in Beverly Hills, one of his mentors whom we adore and who urges us not to elope to Vegas. She cooks a beautiful meal of chile verde, margaritas, and flan. We say our vows in front of her fireplace with a handful of friends and my bouquet from an off-ramp flower stand. Afterwards, someone plays "Wonderful Tonight" on their phone and so we dance for a moment, just Ryan and me, circling again to the song even further from its era now, one we still don't love but that's somehow ours.

✧

[*That gold? Its particles are so minuscule that you can't collect it, can't touch it. You can't see it at all—not even a sheen or glimmer.*]

On a recent summer walk in our neighborhood, I ask Ryan, "Do you believe in marriage? Do you think it's important that we did it, the actual, official thing?" It's an institution with which I'll never fully square myself. And yet.

He considers it for a moment.

"No, not really," he says in his unbothered, thoughtful way before nudging our dog, Jack, down the path. And I feel again like the woman in the shop who met the man who also saw the skull.

David Berman passed away last year, a loss we observed by returning to his songs and poems on hot summer nights. Ryan revisited the correspondence he shared with him over the years, cartoons Berman scrawled and mailed, the time he mentioned "a friend" in an interview and the friend was Ryan. In some ways: the end of an era. But I also question the notion of beginnings and endings, of straight lines or clear shots, or the idea that a person could stray off course if she tried. Life loops like waves, those circles with their own logic and timing. It's enough to make you feel stupid. Or to wade out to your knees in belief.

GRACELAND, 1994

Cobain died. Kurt Loder told us in a Memphis Days Inn on spring break. Family vacation. My brother and I on the edge of an unmade bed, blackout curtains blocking the parking lot. Shotgun, Loder said. "Blast to the head." The electrician who discovered the scene phoned a radio station before calling the cops. We knew every lyric. Guitar: my brother's new language. Me? I had gallons of desire and an ounce of despair, so I filled the pages of a diary with the ocean on it. The Lemonheads and Pixies, Fugazi and Sunspring. Nirvana, our first CD, now every rare B-side. "Marigold" my favorite. "About a Girl"? I didn't want to be her. I knew it was no love song—just crumbs from a shitty boyfriend. I wanted to sing, not be sung to. I'd rather have been Kurt and gave my bleached hair his same cut in my dresser mirror. My brother wore duct tape on his shoes. We wore shabby thrift store sweaters that embarrassed my father. The chipper bow in my baby sister's hair signaled a different generation. Back home beneath my bedroom Christmas lights, I'd painted other lyrics on my walls: Tori Amos, Fiona Apple, Hole. Courtney forever in her white satin slip dress and ruby lipstick, baby on her hip. She'd read his suicide note to fans standing in the rain while the internet remained a daydream. I'd drive soon. I'd live in a dorm room at the state school. My body made of water, what didn't I want when I climbed out the basement window at midnight? My brother and I wanted to stay in the hotel room all day, tuned to channel thirty-nine. We wanted a vigil with cheap cherry wax candles. My dad drove us down the street to Graceland. Lush spring outside our family minivan and the shotgun blast so bleak that I closed my eyes and leaned my head back against the seat. We bought tour tickets. Living room, jungle room, dining room with blue velvet curtains and perfect place settings. Staff must dust each day, those plates and glasses behind stanchions. Like our ordinary table at home where our spots waited for us, already a relic.

WHEN THE GUN COMES

Born bulletless, a mark of privilege: no need for defense, no use for weapons in our desert or suburb or Kentucky county, no interest in them. Our family's men? No hunters or sport shooters. Our boys? No BB guns, no air rifles. No risk of getting shot by nervous cops who couldn't see the orange plastic tip on the end of a toy barrel because cops didn't occupy our neighborhoods. Less risk because of the color of our skin. Guns meant zero to us, to me. All I knew at first: our great uncle Buster, Frances's wild brother who'd shot two fingers off in an accident, then put them in a cooler and drove them to the hospital on the back of his motorcycle. Doctors couldn't reattach them, and as a young kid, I'd wonder at this serious, gritty man when he visited her living room.

Then the first gun I knew about, fourth grade: I didn't hear it, didn't see it, but got ordered indoors and abandoned my scooter in the driveway of our suburban split-level. This was a mandate to my mother via phone or neighbor. Panic pulsed in my chest as I waited inside with my best friend on my daybed with the boom-box loud to drown out whatever we weren't supposed to hear.

A high school student had shot his ex-girlfriend at the nearby video store where she worked and he now barricaded himself in our neighbor's bathroom. Cops threatened tear gas. Did I hear bullhorns? Did I ask my mom why the boy did it or did I know the girl had broken up with him? I could hardly fathom the death of a teenager, that apex of maturity and beauty and freedom. I thought about the girl behind the cash register we'd stood in line at so often, popcorn popping and candy boxes stocked at the checkout counter. The homeowners who were gone when he broke in would return soon to find this tense, grim scene, the cop cars in their driveway, lights swirling, while this kid hid behind a shower curtain. No one had to tell me that the girl died. I don't remember if the boy died, too.

On the radio: the old Atlantic Starr song "Always." The lyrics made me queasy, the sappy back-and-forth of a man and woman professing eternal love. It was corny, creepy—even to young me with zero understanding of romance. Could the same man who'd call a radio station and have this song dedicated to a woman be the same kind of person who'd hurt her?

My mom eventually released us to the front yard, but the sun had set beyond the twisted oak trees. Somewhere in this same dusk, two separate families grieved while my own ate take-out pizza on a Friday night. My friend stayed for a sleepover, the two of us watching television on the sofa bed in the living room, unable to sleep.

◣◢◤

The only gun I've shot is a .22 rifle my grandfather brought to the backyard for my brothers and me because it's a desert pastime to blast rusted cans against fences or riddle abandoned cars in the piñon hills. I was twelve. My grandfather arranged targets, coached our aim. He chuckled at, then corrected me, when I gripped it like a machine gun and braced for heavy kickback because I only knew guns from movies. Thirty minutes maybe and that was it: I never shot the gun or even saw it again and I'm not sure my brothers did either—none of us cared, plus who could have fun beneath my grandfather's eye and picky instruction? We'd rather read, rockhound, draw, listen to music. Even this weapon that hadn't left the shed in a decade had no place in our imaginations.

The other guns? There's L., my childhood friend who'd lived up the street, a boy who'd sleep over and volley water balloons and swim at Topaz Lake with me for long summer days while our moms talked in beach chairs and our siblings played: he was thirteen when his friend showed him his parent's gun, a quick act that killed him. By then our family had moved to Kentucky. When my mom relayed the news, it stormed outside in heavy gusts above the woods and I went up to my bedroom and flipped through the few photos I had of him. I hadn't seen him for years, couldn't imagine him older now, a kid I'd want to kiss maybe. Who would his family be without him, the freckled brother and sister on either side, his temperamental dad, his gentle, dark-haired mom laughing for hours next to mine with her feet in the lake water?

And there was D. when I was fifteen, D. hanging out after school with friends when he thought the gun was empty and, according to the story, held it to his head as a joke. Then that was it: he was gone, over like a poem, and a counselor waited in the school office and girls wept on their boyfriend's flannel shirts near the lockers and some of us held hands in our parents' minivans that drove us to the overfull evening memorial in the Crestwood church next to the Little League field. People remembered him for how sweet he was, worried over his girlfriend who'd witnessed it, circulated grainy photocopies of the "Do Not Stand at My Grave and Weep" poem and played Pink Floyd's "Wish You Were Here" in their cars as they got high in the IGA parking lot after school. Then a blizzard pummeled our town, canceling school for a week, and so we traveled winding, perilous country roads to hang out in one another's basements, making out sometimes but mostly lighting incense and listening to the Pixies and Jane's Addiction and the Grateful Dead as snow piled up on empty cornfields, all of us mournful and amazed that someone our age could be here and then gone in an actual, literal second.

\/﹀

My grandfather's gun story isn't just our story, because there were others present at Carson Tahoe Hospital that morning. If anything, it's more theirs than ours: we weren't there, we didn't hear the noise echo down the halls. Our reckoning is personal yet secondhand.

Regardless of my grandfather's intention, I consider the hearts stopped at the sound of the single shot, the psyches jarred, the people who thought, if even for a second, that they should run or take cover, who thought, *This is it*. The nurses and staff, the doctors and custodians, the patients resting or immobile in neighboring rooms, the parents with children in tow visiting relatives, the volunteers: Frances had actually served as a hospital volunteer for many years, delivering flowers and shiny balloons to new mothers. I picture these people frozen in fear, tossing in their beds that night, rightfully angry, nervous now in certain public spaces.

In the seconds after Mallory first called me—those crystalline moments like ice breaking beneath my feet—I felt much more than grief and panic. "He did WHAT?" were the first words from my mouth, because who does something like this, in America, today? I've often thought of those people affected by my grandfather's decision, felt tethered to them. I've wanted to say that I'm sorry. I'm sorry.

Since I started writing this piece three weeks ago, at least three mass shootings have occurred in our country. Those are the ones I can count, but there are probably more, and the tally becomes tricky. Sometimes when Ryan and I walk at night, our dog, Jack, between us, we share details from our days and talk about the news and the news is often guns. Sometimes it's so many different guns that we get confused: Was this the shooting with the white nationalist or the other guy with the manifesto? The school with multiple killings or the one where there were only injuries?

Since I finished that small paragraph above, US cops foiled three mass shooting attempts in a single weekend. We now live in an age when a shooting survivor might go on to survive a second mass shooting at a concert or bar or small-town food festival. The math becomes complicated and this essay can't keep up.

My grandfather didn't shoot strangers or inflict violence out of rage, didn't intentionally terrorize anyone. But he demonstrated how easily he could've done just that if he'd wanted to, how easily he could've taken others' lives along with Frances's, if even by accident. He drove to a store and bought a gun like he might have bought a drill or one of the short-sleeve collared shirts in his closet. Should it have been so simple? Should he have had to answer more questions at the counter or wait a day or two?

Sometimes I think, *Guns and gun violence have nothing to do with our family. Isn't this a stretch?* But then I remember that my grandmother was shot, a bullet through her abdomen or chest, depending which report you read. Her death certificate lists it as the cause. The news stories did, too. So did the hospital, which publicly announced changes to its safety policies as a result of the incident one year later.

↘↙

There's the sea, Frances's Pacific, or the Gulf of Mexico back east, a place of joyful memories, where I swam on family vacations in my cold, goose-bumped skin, my body buoyant, the sun glittering on the surface of the water and warming the top of my head.

Or barefoot on the back lawn at my mom's house, which was Bill and Frances's house, pink sun inking the desert at dusk, all of us gathered for dinner, taking silly selfies with our faces pressed against one another's, my nephews and niece filling plastic buckets with water to build something in the sand, eating my mom's enchiladas in a lawn chair, a slice of cake on a paper plate as the evening chills.

Or at home with Ryan, sitting on the back deck at dusk, wondering why someone would plant a decorative plum tree in the backyard, sticky plums you can't eat but have to collect from the yard, more plums falling even when you think the season has ended, plums in perpetuity, beautiful and useless at sunset.

Or in bed at night, me awake as he sleeps, the neighbors asleep, too, a solitary train whistling west in the city, the desert alive beyond these streets and buildings, pronghorn and coyotes, everything a still, breathing miracle.

It's not hopeless—there are still places without guns.

TRANSCRIPT: HITCHHIKERS

BILL DRESSER: I always remember the old Venice rollercoaster. That was a big deal. I mean, I never rode it—I was a kid—but I'd hear that son of a gun *go*. We'd lay in the sand there—that hot old sand—and doze off and hear that rollercoaster and as it was going up it'd kind of *click-click-click-click-click* and it'd get to the top and down it'd go and you'd hear all these people, "*Ahhhhh.*" [*Laughs.*]

FRANCES DRESSER: You know, a big treat for me and my siblings is when my dad would drive us up to Griffith Observatory. And, boy, you could just look out all over and it was clear.

BD: You know, my parents did the same thing. Everything was so clear. No smog or fog.

ASHLEY FARMER: Where the observatory is?

BD: Yeah. We never went in it, but they had a nice place where you could stand and view the whole city. I remember my mom taking my sister and I to the, uh—what was that tallest building in Los Angeles? City Hall! Yeah. We'd go up in the top of that thing and look around.

FD: I used to tell younger kids, "That's the tallest building in the United States." Far from it [*laughs*]. I think the Broadway was as tall as it!

AF: [*Laughs.*] When you talk about the Venice Pier, that's different from the Santa Monica Pier?

BD: Yes. Santa Monica Pier is pretty much like it was back then.

AF: There's a Ferris wheel and there's a little rollercoaster, but that's not the same one you're talking about, right?

BD: Santa Monica Pier, they had one of those merry-go-rounds. Remember that, merry-go-rounds?

FD: That was a big deal.

BD: And I'd go down there. We had a boat—I was in the Sea Scouts and we had a boat and we put it in the water and had a lot of fun with that. One time we really got carried away: there were three of us in the boat, it was overloaded, and we went out around the old Billings barge—it was a fishing barge out there. This guy was sailing it and two of us were bailing water just to keep from sinking [*laughs*].

FD: You know what I can remember way back when? My dad worked for the Greyhound and he'd buy a fifty-pound bag of potatoes and of course he didn't have a car, so he was taking the streetcar back and forth to work. And he would buy a fifty-pound sack and bring some home on the streetcar every day from his work.

BD: I remember my dad coming home from work and I'd get in his lunch pail to see if there was anything I could get. He'd have an avocado in there and it'd be like two or three days and he'd say yeah, you can have it [*laughs*].

FD: Every other Friday, we'd walk down to the top of the hill and watch my dad get off the streetcar and that was four blocks. And if he had a white bag, we knew he'd stopped at the sweet shop and bought a whole bunch of candy and the bag would be that tall. In a way, you know, it's kind of nice to be poor. You appreciate the smaller things. But in another way, it's really shitty [*laughs*] because you don't get a lot of the smaller things.

BD: I think of all the slack my parents gave me.

FD: I think they were trying to get rid of you, myself!

BD: Well, Russell and I decided we was gonna take off.

FD: And how old were you?

BD: Probably about thirteen. Thirteen or fourteen.

FD: Jesus Christ!

AF: And Russell is your . . . ?

BD: My buddy. My friend. So we hitchhiked all the way to San Francisco and—

FD: Did your parents ever tell you not to hitchhike?

BD: Probably. I don't know.

FD: I can remember my parents telling my brothers.

BD: We walked—I guess we might have been a little bit older than that because they had antiaircraft guns set up on the Golden Gate Bridge—and we walked all the way across the bridge and back.

AF: Oh, my gosh.

BD: And we spent the night there in Coit Tower, which is a kind of an attraction-place. We slept in there. We were pretty hungry, you know. I think Russell had a few bucks, but I don't think I had much. We were walking down the street there in San Francisco and we smelled this bread, this bakery, and it was like you go downstairs to go into it. And we went down there to see if we could buy a loaf of bread. Couldn't find anybody in that bakery! That thing was going full bore and everything's smelling so good and we couldn't find anybody so we got ourselves a loaf of bread and left.

He had an aunt who lived in Visalia, so we started hitchhiking from there and it was cold and we slept at night and I don't think we had any bedding or anything—we just froze our little tails off—and the next day we was still hitchhiking and I think we was looking kind of rough—I think we needed to shave, you know—and it started raining and we were wet as dogs and we weren't that far from his aunt and uncle's and this guy picked us up. He was a farmer, and he was going that way and we rode there and when we got there, oh, they treated us so nice—oh, God—put us in a nice bed and it was warm and cozy and we got to take a shower or bath and we stayed there a couple of days and they had a nice farm and I remember you could walk down between the rows of the tomatoes and pick them off and they were really good eatin'. And they got us all shined up and then we took off and hitchhiked home. But it was quite an ordeal.

AF: How long were you gone?

BD: I think about four or five days. Oh, yeah, surely.

FD: He had a lot more leeway than me.

BD: We spent a night in San Francisco, then we spent a night in the country between Frisco and where his aunt and uncle was. I remember he had a Model A Ford and he let us drive it.

FD: All I ever remember—well, not *all* I remember—was my mom telling the boys, "Don't go over in that railroad yard." So you know where they headed.

BD: Another big deal is when the ice truck came down the street. Back then, you know, you had a card you'd put in your window. It was like twenty, twenty-five, thirty, fifty, and if you wanted twenty-five pounds of ice you'd turn it to where the twenty-five was up and the ice man would come bring you twenty-five pounds of ice for your icebox and it was a big deal because he had all these ice chips and the kids would be there grabbing these ice chips—

FD: You'd think you were getting ice *cream*! [*Laughs.*] Just ice chips—oh, boy!

BD: Especially nice on a hot day.

FD: I felt bad when that—I can't think of his name (I thought of it a few minutes ago)—he got killed during the war.

ANIMAL HOURS

Anxious me on the long couch at five a.m., the spook hour with a moon slit between palm trees. It's the fear that makes my bones shake, that makes me wretch my morning guts up. *The fear* being anxiety that's beyond anxiety: the fear that's electricity, burning my armpits, balled up in my throat. I can't drink coffee even at this hour with a film of darkness shrouding ghosts, can't gag extra adrenaline. Eat? That's haha-funny, when I'm lucky if I can breathe.

Ryan: in the bedroom, swimming through dreams.

Me? Caught alone in a squeeze.

See, he doesn't sense our apartment spinning and our life unseaming, each thread ripping out. Long Beach where we live far from family is wired weird and worse: this way that we make our living, teaching college classes as adjuncts, worried whether we'll have jobs next semester, month, week. Will they need us? Will we have rent money? If not, where will we go? I never know if I'm teaching until I take first day attendance because these schools snag classes back a week before the semester begins. On weekends, I lead language courses for children at an office park and tutor in gated community mansions, drilling spelling words and dissecting *Little Women* in palaces with personal chefs and white marble floors.

So this is the catch: we live in this city for our jobs but our jobs aren't actually jobs and we couldn't have picked a trickier town to scrape up a living. We love teaching—we want nothing *but* to teach—but it's a tightrope and if we trip, we're finished.

No more savings, no safety net. No insurance for me until that November when we quickly marry, so when I go running to eke out serotonin, I slow myself down the stairs (don't want to trip and break my teeth).

Meditate. Replace fear with trust. What I trust is that we must leave this place now, but go where? We should quit this line of work but do what? Sunk cost fallacy, this path: I think, *Just a little longer*, getting paid nothing but hoping that, this time, so much nothing transforms into something secure. So in the thin skin of morning I play YouTube clips of New Age gurus whose voices soothe, and then I climb in bed, curling against Ryan's back. He stays asleep until I whisper, "I have the fear," which, right now, is how I often wake him up.

Our apartment building has a copper-colored tile courtyard and a fountain that gurgles. Fuchsia bougainvillea blooms and plump figs plop onto the ground. When a friend visits us, he looks around and says, "You're doing alright." His approval is a balm, but our life in California is a Rorschach test: Look one way and there's pristine sea to infinity, the twinkling coast dotted with piers. Look the other way and it's the guy outside the reptile shop karate-kicking a tree. One way: scenic beach where they're filming Disney kids' shows beneath rainbow umbrellas. Another way and the cops return on Thanksgiving for the downstairs lady who threatens to kill a stranger with a brass lamp.

Rorschach Example B: our apartment looks tidy, comfortable, clean, and so our visiting friend wouldn't know about the termite game. Here's how you play: sit stone-still in a rolling chair and watch for the termites' skitters across the floor. When you spot them crawling, affix clear masking tape over the cracks they crawled from, sweep the bugs up, scatter them outside. Notice how they spin on their backs, the ones with wings. Over months, the floor gleams with tape while the building foundation erodes. An infestation isn't something you see unless the floors collapse—a possibility that occurs to us with every barefoot creak.

I'm also infected with the invisible: this anxiety, this adrenaline thing. I'm also the inkblot test. See, after I peel away from Ryan, I ready myself: black dress, makeup, hair fixed, final swipe of pink lipstick. In the mirror I look calm, but inside I'm a mess. I take the I-710 to the Vincent Thomas Bridge toward one of the campuses where I teach, my soundtrack a guru's mantra and podcasts about managing stress with mindfulness. By the time I park my car and carry stacks of graded essays to our classroom, you'd almost believe me, pretending to be a legitimate teacher. Pretending to be an adult with an actual job. Some students even call me *professor*, which I'm not.

I've always been conscious of beginnings, and endings are what any writer observes—those litanies of lasts. But sensing the beginning of the end is trickier, and I can say only now that's what the animal hour is: the moment before things break. Before we're finished, done.

◣╱◂

But before that, Ryan and I collect quick joys. After all, we live in California near friends, other adjuncts only blocks away, and so summer nights we crowd the pub that's made to look like a church or the wine bar with cheap deals for teachers on Monday nights during the school year. And there's the basketball season when our hometown team plows through the National Championship and our friends gather on our hand-me-down couches to cheer over guacamole and chips. We throw Kentucky Derby shindigs, walk to potlucks down Second Street, hot dishes in arms and six-pack handles in fists. We drive two hours to a golden sunlit field to watch a pair we adore marry. And love, yes, that has us, too: we're together after three years of grad school long distance. We soak in Los Angeles when we we're not teaching or grading and there are heaps of pinch-me moments as I ride passenger side at golden hour near the white letters of the Hollywood sign, the light and road and love by my side beautiful enough to make me cry. See, life in California isn't a catastrophe, and anyway: I was born here, though I moved away as a baby, and so was my mother and so was her mother, and I sense my ties to this place, swell with an affinity, and I can will myself to think that—adjunct nonsense be damned—our living here is a good thing.

Even though we're mostly broke and our time mostly accounted for, we splurge sometimes, drinking more than we ought to, nipping straight tequila in the good glasses we inherited as we prep classes late into the night. It's both self-medication and symbolic indulgence: we might not have actual jobs, might sense the foundation breaking beneath us, so we do what we please, play pretend at middle class. Other pastimes are free: we walk together, up the shore, past the *Queen Mary* anchored at rest, or the other way past Cherry Park where our neighborhood morphs into the pricy one. We memorize the houses and what they contain: the ferocious red living room with a white baby grand, the David Lynchian glass cube, the castle with its intense turrets, the meth-lab mansion they demolished in two days even though it looked million-dollar inhabitable.

We discuss leaving, plot to escape the Golden State and our less-than-professional professions: pack up the Isuzu, crate the cat, be back to Louisville in three days. Find jobs? We could do it, could work any steady gigs that'd have us, plus our family there wouldn't let us go roofless, would make room for us. We're lucky in this way, for the luxury of knowing we'd survive. We have heaps of privilege. We're healthy. It could be so, so much worse. (These are the other mantras, the other truths, I mouth out loud and in my brain on repeat.)

Other times, when we get optimistic, we float the idea of having a kid.

"Should we?" I ask Ryan.

"Maybe," he says.

At thirty-three, I feel a buzzy joy at the thought of a baby. It could be destiny, this tiny being that might meteor into our lives, so we talk through the easy stuff: I'll take prenatal vitamins, we'll start trying in a couple of months. But anything beyond that seems absurd: How could we afford a bigger apartment? Childcare? There's no chance of balancing our schedules since we must take the schedules they give us. Do we want to walk this tightrope with a baby in tow? Is it fair to us, to him or her? No security, no prospects of anything steady. A few blocks further and we again see this hope for what it is: something we can't yet pull off. And so the conversation fades as the sunset dims and we walk home, the two of us, to Termite City.

\/-

So what's the marker, when's the first tilt? Where do things slide sideways for me? Maybe it's the moment I'm in Costa Mesa so overwhelmed with actual work and especially the fear of lack of work that I drive away from the gas station with the pump stuck inside our VW's gas tank. Or the time I become convinced I left a stack of student essays at one campus and so I drive forty minutes back to that school and sit outside the door for two hours until someone else's class empties out into the night only to find that the papers aren't there, maybe never were, maybe exist only as a ghost stack among many actual stacks from any one of the various places where I teach. Maybe it's the moment when the administrator makes the uncomfortable remark to me on the first day of the semester. Maybe it's when I see a doctor and mention my panicked heart and he asks me to write myself an antidepressant prescription—"What kind do you want?"—and because I don't know, I slip out squinting into the parking lot empty-fisted. These are the initial blips and rattles. This is the hand nearing my throat.

And, see, it's not just us who's stressed, not just me sensing my unsteady place in this world: our neighbor, an IT guy with two pit bulls and a street bike, gets hooked on something or something hooks into him. Across two months, his face morphs, his clothes droop. One Sunday afternoon when we're grading and watching the Saints trounce the Cowboys on our tiny television, we hear a loud *pop-pop-pop* and my first thought is a palm tree snapping in the courtyard. Our neighbor is firing a gun into our shared storage space and shouting, "I didn't want it to come to this!" Cops arrive almost instantly with their weapons drawn. They yell, "Put the gun down!" They scream and wait.

Time slows, goes gluey. Ryan and I are afraid that we're about to see him, this neighbor we know, killed right in front of us.

"I don't have a gun!" he says, holding his weapon high above his head like he's forgotten—and he's likely forgotten because he's high out of his mind.

It's a miracle, really, how the officers demonstrate restraint and we're relieved to see our neighbor surrender. That night, his ex-girlfriend collects the dogs from his first-floor lighted rooms with bent blinds and she tells us about her ex's recent paranoia (he thought the CIA installed cameras to spy on him and conspired to starve his dogs while, at the same time, the ghost of his dead sister haunted him. This is why he'd shot into the storage closet: he thought his deceased sister was trapped and he tried to shoot her out). We climb into bed jacked up and rattled and Ryan finds the booking shot online. "Rest easy," Ryan says. "There's no chance he'll be back tonight. His bail is sky-high."

I barely sleep just the same and the next morning it's off to campus after campus.

The exodus begins. Many of our friends leave Southern California, scattering to temporary teaching gigs in Indiana, Minnesota, Hong Kong, further up the coast. It feels like we've stayed too long: the sitcom era—youngish professionals in a seaside city—has ended. I'd clung to that illusion in an era filled with them. Like how one night, I learn about the Long Beach breakwaters, submerged walls that hold the water in and keep the waves out. It's the reason the ocean is placid where we live, its surface so still. But it wasn't always like this—vintage pictures from my grandparents' era show men posed with surfboards, waves crashing behind them.

I drive alone to Nevada to see my family and once I'm through the three-hour traffic slog I slip so swiftly through the desert night that I don't know how fast I'm going. A cop catches me, slaps me a ticket, and it's a huge one because it was almost one hundred miles per hour, this speed, this sailing, nearly the kind of fast that gets you locked in desert jail. I'm shaking when I call Ryan from the side of the road to tell him, but he's sweet about it, if not incredulous and slightly pissed because it'll be expensive and he's the slower driver, not amped up the way I am. The ticket feels like a referendum on my character because I'm usually a rule follower, although I've gotten disillusioned with rules, come to think of it.

I'm only a few more miles down the road when a neighbor calls me, a neighbor who normally wouldn't call me, and never at this hour, so I suspect something's weird in the building, maybe the kookier neighbors riled up and rowdy. Instead, she says, "Ryan's okay but he got jumped."

I don't get it, can't quite grasp what she's getting at, and so she explains that a group of guys beat him outside our courtyard gates. I ask to talk to him, to hear proof that he's alright, and his voice sounds dejected and fed up, not frantic like I'd expect. He needs stitches, has a concussion, isn't allowed to sleep. They busted his glasses. His wedding ring flew into the bushes, something a cop helped him find in the dark. He'd refused the ambulance they brought because of cost but they made him promise to go to the hospital with this neighbor, our friend, made him swear it. Only later will I see the picture she shot on her phone: Ryan beaten beneath the streetlamp, so much blood, eyebrow split, dark red soaking the red button-up he'd worn to teach in that day.

No license plate on the idling car. No way to catch them. They only stopped beating him because Ryan yelled up to our neighbor's open window and she, this adjunct teacher like us, ran toward the mess, screaming and scaring them off.

"You got lucky," one cop told him. "It doesn't usually end this well. But be careful, because they could come back to finish the job."

✕

Most things don't happen as we plan, but the day we exit California unfolds like what we'd talked about on walks: we pack what fits in our cars, sweep the floor a final time, corral the protesting cat in her crate, set the GPS back to Louisville, Kentucky. The bare apartment gleams, tape gone: we leave it cleaner than when we arrived. The sun shines that morning because it shines more often than not, that seventy-degrees-and-sunny cliché largely true. But we feel no sentimentality, only readiness, eager to abandon these rooms to someone else's California chapter.

My grandparents ditched Los Angeles in the 1970s when, long after the streetcars and orange groves vanished, the pace overwhelmed them. My parents followed suit when I, their first kid, was five months old: my mom saw a person shot on the ground outside their Garden Grove apartment building and when she commiserated with the stranger next to her, cops ran up and arrested the guy she was talking to for the murder. Yet the photo albums I sifted through as a kid—pages I'd memorized for both their history and what my own future might look like—all took place in California. Like my grandparents in the tidy backyard of their first home. My dad and my eight-months-pregnant mom curled up on a mattress with my dad's homemade birthday cake between them, candles lit. Me as an infant in a pink bikini, ears newly pierced, snoozing under the lifeguard tower during my first trip to the beach.

As Ryan and I drive away, I start to discard these eras not from memory but as my own desires. It's when I begin to scrap that pursuit of a life my parents and grandparents made: something linear, nuclear. It's also when I stop trying for academic gigs. What to call grief that's lightness? Mourning that's relief? There ought to be a name for this feeling, something I try to pin down as I follow Ryan's truck on the freeway. Despite our careful planning to leave post–rush hour, traffic is gridlocked, our packed cars idling in a six-lane artery. Ahead of us: a car on fire, flames at the side of the road. It takes us hours to maneuver through the city and it's funny, almost, California's final prank on us: fire and smoke in our rearview mirror.

\/◂

I've only seen double rainbows once in my life and I promise you this: it was driving on the Vincent Thomas Bridge. I tried to photograph them out my window as I steered and it was raining and I'd wanted them to show up on my phone the way they looked in real life as I sailed high above the barges and the black-blue water made choppy from a rare storm. I drove alone, commuting home from school, but I wished for a witness. The gurus might call it karma for driving one-handed and not being careful, because the colors didn't show up in the photos, not so much as a hint. Which made me wonder if I'd imagined the scene, whether the rainbows were all in my head. Would it be so bad? There were worse things to imagine, and I had imagined them.

It was almost the same spot soon before we moved where I'd stall in traffic on the bridge: a first for me. Totally stopped midway, I marveled at the heavy cables and bolts of this death-defying contraption and a lump built in my throat as I sensed just how high I was above the Pacific. I felt exhilarated, almost dizzy, to be suspended in the air like that.

TRANSCRIPT: SHIPYARD

ASHLEY FARMER: So, you were right by the bridges?

BILL DRESSER: Yeah, that one was called St. Vincent?

AF: Yeah, the Vincent Thomas Bridge.

BD: I mean, originally there wasn't any bridge: they had ferries going back and forth there. And the only bridge we had was called the Ford Bridge. You know where that is? It's the only one that opens up.

AF: Like a drawbridge?

BD: Yeah. And then there was another small bridge that they replaced. They called it a pontoon bridge. It was the closest one to Long Beach. You'd come down Ocean Avenue and you go right onto that pontoon bridge and on to Terminal Island. Two ways to get on there during the war: the Ford Bridge and the pontoon bridge.

AF: And you saw the *Queen Mary*?

BD: Saw it? You bet.

AF: That's right by where we live now. And it's been there since when you last saw it?

BD: Right. When it left our shipyard, that's where it went. They actually did all the work to put it over there. I've got pictures of it that I took while I was on the ship. They sandblasted the whole thing—we had it dried out—sandblasted the whole bottom and put on some real, real anticorrosive paint so that it would last a long time. They took off the propellers and I think they enclosed one some way so people could look at it.

I was on that thing all by myself one time. More than once.

AF: You were on it in the very end?

BD: Yeah, I saw it come in.

AF: And that boat was a big deal at the time, wasn't it?

BD: It was the largest ship in the world. They had the *Normandy*, the *Queen Mary* was English, and they were the two biggest ships at the time. The *Normandy* caught fire in New York—feel like it was sabotage. But anyway, all we had was the *Queen Mary*. The *Queen Mary* was used to transport troops back and forth during World War II.

AF: Did you like your work at the shipyard?

BD: Did I like working there?

AF: Yeah, did you like what you did on a day-to-day basis?

BD: I liked it when I was a mechanic. But I didn't like being a supervisor.

AF: You liked more of the physical work?

BD: I don't like dealing with other personalities, other people's problems. Drunks or whatever. I had to fire a couple of them.

AF: But the work, the actual work on the boats—

BD: Oh, I loved it—I loved it, yeah. I did such a good job, they made me a supervisor [*laughs*].

AF: [*Laughs.*] "Thanks a lot."

BD: The pay was a lot better.

AF: That's the catch, huh?

BD: Didn't have to punch in a timecard, or punch it to come out. But I had everyone else's timecards to deal with. I had a supervisor who was a drunk—it didn't make my job any easier.

AF: Was it all men? There were probably no women, huh?

BD: Just starting. We passed some kind of deal and these girls in the office couldn't get ahold of an application fast enough to file for a man's job and get more pay.

AF: It seems like it would definitely be male dominated.

BD: Yeah. I never had any women in my crew. But just about the time I was leaving, that was happening.

AF: When did you leave?

BD: I left the shipyard in 1976. I had thirty years of service.

THREE

NEVADA / ST. TROPEZ, 1987

What miraculous energy. Mine, I mean. Like how my legs with growing pains ache at night for the grape-flavored aspirin on my tongue, tiny sacrament. In the bathtub, I skim my shins with my mom's BIC but it's a secret. No nicks. No pink blood in the bubbles that smell like babies or gum. God, I'm ready, but for what? The model from television with wet hair slicked back rises in her black bandeau between scenes from *General Hospital* as though Pygmalion made her for commercial breaks. She lounges poolside. The ocean glows behind her. A man in a tux brings her Bain de Soleil, the same orange tanning gel in our cabinet: it smells like glamour even by our plastic backyard pool. She refuses to smile. Her face reads *relaxed*. But I'm urgent: to search the piñon hills for mine shafts. To wear sequined tights beneath stage lights. To jump from the high backyard fence in hopes that I become somebody before I land. I've studied the clear plastic pages inside Frances's anatomy book. Page of muscles, page of veins, page of naked, cartoon bones—only together do they add up to something. Make me add up, to sit atop a pale, distant cliff in my grown skin where I don't have to grin. Take me away like how my dad sings "Sailing" at the Weber grill out back, torching T-bones over charcoal as hot wind whips the dress shirt my mother bought him on clearance. Take me away like Calgon beneath the bathroom sink. Because we'll throw horseshoes in the yard tonight, each winning throw ringing the stake. I'll bury my bare feet in the dirt and pull goat-heads from my heels. And still: I want to be dustless and pristine, like the satin-suited doll who comes to life in *Mannequin*. I want to be Sloane with Ferris Bueller at the art museum, glamorous and grown and finally in on a secret.

BODY COMPOSITION

1.

Women have more taste buds than men. The color blue is an appetite suppressant. People really do "eat with their eyes first." 91 percent of women are dissatisfied with their bodies. One-third of the people who say they diet normally actually have a pathological approach to it. Hunger is biological while appetite is psychological.

Spring afternoons, Frances slips through our front door, rose lipstick and blush, the scent of Giorgio on her neck, and she kisses me with a *Hi, sweetheart!* before heading to the kitchen for a pot of Folgers with my mom. I'm six and she lives next door. In my grandmother's fist: a haul of ice creams, pastel soft-serve frozen like rocks in Styrofoam cups—fake strawberry flavor, faker banana, vanilla, chocolate—and if I'm lucky, I'll get to chip at one while I watch afternoon cartoons. These treats arrive from Weight Watchers and even though the sugar tastes aluminumish, sweet is sweet. What does a kindergartener know about a weight-loss program? I picture something vaguely Olympic: a scale, a judge issuing a ribbon or score. But I'm confused because my grandmother is gorgeous—glamorous, even, with the movie-star gap between her front teeth and her pristine leather handbags and the fuchsia uniform she wears as a hospital volunteer. "Isn't she beautiful?" my mother will ask me when Frances isn't around and, yes, of course, I agree.

Frances starts this tradition for my spring birthday when I'm six: casino lunch then bathing suit shopping. It's meant to feel grown-up and fancy, us dining at the Ormsby House buffet with its white-pistol-and-red-rose logo. I love the dangerous sign, the weapon and thorny flower lighted with casino bulbs, and we travel to the top floor seating which feels New York City–cosmopolitan in a way I know only from sitcoms or movies (and because it's Carson City, is only ten floors up). "Eat dessert first!" Frances says. "Eat *only* dessert, if you want." I indulge without shame, plucking frosted brownies and baby-pink cakes from silver trays, and we laugh about being so stuffed that the staff will have to roll us outside like beach balls. I picture bad, blue Violet from *Willy Wonka*, Violet with her appetite and demands—I could never be a kid like that.

Afterwards, we drive an hour to Reno to search out a perfect bathing suit, the main clothing item I'll wear all summer in the backyard desert sprinklers or at Topaz Lake or up at pristine Tahoe with its too-cold, Caribbean-colored water that tinges my lips blue. I choose a ruffled one-piece with a single shoulder strap. Standing nearly naked in the dressing room, I'm not concerned about my body, don't judge its height or weight or shape, don't believe that I should. Inside myself, giddy and sugar-rushed with someone I love most in this world, my body and its joys belong to me.

2.

96 percent of women wouldn't call themselves beautiful. Women will date an average of five men before finding a partner. A mother's ability to respond to her baby's needs impacts the child's nervous system and temperament. In some studies, new parents experienced as great a drop in happiness as the newly divorced, unemployed, or bereaved. Fathers are happier than mothers.

My mother's body? It belongs to me, too.

It belongs to all of us kids, even the borrowed ones she babysits, a chaos of children splashing at a lake's edge, this hooting and shrieking crew she eagle-eyes from her sun-bleached beach towel. I lean against my mother's back with my arms around her neck. Her freckled skin is hot to my cheek and scented with coconut. A gold necklace glints on her chest—this ornate camel charm from before I was born—and I'm mesmerized by this gift from a man who's not our father, a gift of gold, no less, from a life predating us, because who was she before? How could she exist before she made us?

At the end of a lake day, sandy and tan-lined, I sit on the edge of the bathtub as my mom blow-dries her hair, lotions her legs, curls her lashes with the silver tool, and I ask her questions about life before us: Favorite songs and dates? Who did you love before Dad? My mother is a Venus from the Pacific, all Southern California style, her jumpsuits and sandals, her bangles and shell necklaces. I moon over her stories of 1970s LA teens, surfers who ditched their wetsuits in parking lot vans before class, girls who straightened their hair on ironing boards, the twin brothers who drowned in a boat in the ocean together. Rick the Race Car Driver, a guy she dated before my dad. Another guy, the pilot who flew her in his private plane and let it free-fall over Catalina Island, barrel rolls, engines off. Sometimes, she went on two dates in one day: swimming at Huntington Beach with one guy, dancing at the Whisky that night with another. Dizzy to me, heady, this freedom to go wherever you want—to drive and fly and swim in the Pacific and dance beneath lights at a Hollywood club as a woman.

The body if you're a woman. The beauty and strangeness. The

effort and time and transformation. The agency and control, or an approximation. You become your own paradise with mascara and dates and babies, and from my bathtub edge, the view feels both intoxicating and mysterious.

3.

Women experience more anxiety than men. Due to an enzyme deficiency, women can't metabolize alcohol as well as men can.

Backyard bikini days for me the summer we move to Kentucky for my dad's job, the new landscape with the cornfield and dairy farm across the street, the humidity that sucks my breath, our neighbors' warm twangs when they ring our doorbell with poke cake to invite us to their Baptist or Methodist or Episcopal churches. No friends for me yet because it's still summer, but I'm thirteen and there's something about being thirteen: the kid has left my face and I shave my legs and wear a bra I barely need, but still. Outside myself, everything is a signal.

Like the man behind the Dairy Queen window who motions at me with a gesture my parents don't notice and one whose meaning I can only guess. Or at the baseball field where both of my brothers pitch and my sister plays tee ball: inside the steamy concession stand stocked with popcorn and candy, I work my first cash register while a couple of high school guys make dirty jokes outside the window. At home, I water the front yard saplings when the occasional work truck traveling down our country highway honks at me because my body has become a site of appraisal.

We fly that summer, just my brother Brendan and I, back to my grandparents' house for a vacation. These ninety-degree desert weeks snooze by, but they're also a comfort in their childhood familiarity: I memorize Top 40 radio as I lay in the sun out back, visit vintage car shows populated with retirees, go with my grandparents on winding, back seat drives out to Yerington and Hope Valley. Frances's shelves offer paperbacks and I devour a series in which sweater-wearing women bicycle through Scottish fog, drink tea with strangers, then fall in chaste, romantic love. At night, I play backgammon and cribbage with Frances, who keeps score and shows no mercy. Beneath familiar floral bedspreads surrounded by my grandmother's seascapes, I time travel back to being twelve, to just before we moved, suspended in the final flashes of girlhood across weeks of *Jeopardy!* and back porch ice cream bars and fishing in the Truckee River where pine trees sway and rushing water freezes my glittered toenails.

Our legs shake the same, mine and Frances's, a habit that annoys the people sitting next to us, and we talk about it there on the porch swing as night arrives, about being wired that way, the shivering awake in bed at night, heart lodged in the throat. This is the reason for her challenge with alcohol, she says. That's the phrase, *challenge*, because *alcoholism* implies illness, something clinical—someone who can't endure their days or nights without it. We have people like that in our family, too, relatives we've been instructed to never ride with in cars, family who won't leave their homes, people we only know from Polaroids and anecdotes. Though Frances doesn't drink regularly and never around us kids, my mom knows her mother's troubled side, has braced herself against it. "If there's truth in alcohol," my mom said to her, "then you must not like me very much." But my mom regards Frances's struggle with compassion: a glitch in blood or brain, an inheritance from Frances's alcoholic dad, a sickness shared by Frances's sisters who died from it—many in our family have, their sepia lives tinged with addiction and untreated mental illness.

In high school, I'm the kid *Afterschool Specials* were made for: I anticipate overdoses and car wrecks around every corner. I drink just once before college, and it's by accident after junior prom when someone hands me orange juice spiked with vodka as we sit outside on a Kentucky stoop on a humid, buggy night. I love the way booze heats my belly and pricks my brain and makes me crave more. But I resist, because I always resist: when I hang out in snowy hot tubs or in the woods or at the water tower or in basements to watch *The Wall* with friends who are high or tripping. I don't partake, always ready to dial home and get picked up at the end of a gravel driveway or call for help. I observe from the fringe, sober-headed and seat-belted. I watch with the knowledge that, even though it belongs to me, my body's not entirely mine to wield how I want.

4.

Studies suggest that people tend to marry partners who share a similar genetic code. Studies suggest that "couples who sweat together stay together." Women initiate nearly 70 percent of all divorces. According to the CDC, Nevada leads the nation in both marriage rates and divorce.

I'm no winner when it comes to sports, never a true athlete, and yet, at twenty-five, I find myself married to a personal trainer and model-actor who can name every joint and muscle, can detect from across the room if someone's quads are symmetrical. He pursues health trends and I de facto join him: ephedra before the FDA bans it, pricy protein shakes in silver cans, strict hours of treadmills and spin bikes and kettlebells. Weeks pass when our dinners consist of only plain whole wheat spaghetti and beige, broiled chicken breasts. At one point, push-ups become his obsession, push-ups at regular intervals, which means he drops to the ground wherever he happens to be when his alarm rings: crowded airports, friends' living rooms, the small patch of lawn outside a restaurant where we meet his parents for brunch. Toward the end of our marriage, he and I get jobs coaching gymnastics together and, at the women's circuit training gym next door, I also teach aerobics and abs classes. I'm stronger than I've ever been, yet, married to this man, I wonder if I could be better, fitter, more disciplined? It's cruel to ask him this, but I do. "Yes," he says after hedging, rightfully resentful that I'd make him say out loud that there's always room for improvement.

As our marriage disintegrates, my body is how I first rebel. I start smoking after chasing children and training for ten hours, the thinnest I've been since high school, muscles sore, the red gym polo shirt hanging on my back and kids' songs like "Shake Your Sillies Out" banging around in my brain. Sometimes, at the end of a gym shift, I order a large cheese from the Pizza Factory next door and haul it home in my coaching uniform. After bronchitis levels me for weeks, I grow accustomed to slugging from a bottle of Robitussin tucked in my gym bag; my sickness ends, but I take it for longer than I need to just to feel numbish to our marriage's failure, to working fifty-plus hours per week—training bodies, spotting bodies, catching bodies flying from high bars, pushing my own.

We decide to divorce. I move into my mom's house down the road, then throw my back out during a girls' trampoline class. If I can lower myself without debilitating pain, I soak in the bathtub to get relief, crying into the Epsom water, wondering what I'll do next, feeling pathetic and figuring that, among more significant reasons, this breakup is because I married someone with greater physical and mental discipline. I feel bested even though, deep down, I know divorce can't be about the body, about losing an unspoken, unwinnable competition. But still, I smoke cigarettes on my mom's picnic table, sucking nicotine beneath the poplar trees, popping painkillers, feeling sore and sorry for myself and rudderless.

5.

The largest and deepest ocean on Earth is the Pacific, which covers sixty thousand miles and has an average depth of thirteen thousand feet. Our bodies are two-thirds water. Sad tears and happy tears look different from each other. Women cry more than men. Women have more pain receptors than men, but also a higher tolerance for pain. The Buddha said, "I teach only suffering and the end of suffering."

My mom cuts her calf when I'm in high school, slices deep and clean to pink muscle with a hunk of broken glass from a kitchen accident. It's a wound for the ER, no question about it, but she wipes the blood, tapes the gash, goes on carrying out the trash. She'll never visit the doctor for this. If there's a drop of physical resilience in me, it comes from her genes, which are also Frances's genes, their instinct to push despite a cut or cough, to keep physical care of others without seeking more than simple remedies for themselves. Yet I know I'm not cut from this same cloth.

As us kids get older, my mom returns to the water: her Kentucky bathroom has a giant tub, a luxury, and she keeps a stack of books on its edge: spiritual texts and self-help tomes, their pages crinkled with droplets. Water is a conductor and this is where she meditates for hours. Outside the bathroom, she studies Reiki with Catholic nuns and yoga with a mysterious teacher who scolds students by making them stand in corners. We go to a New Age conference where Kirlian photographers take photos of our auras, where healers exchange research, where people who've been clinically dead but came back to life talk about the other side's comfort and brightness. My mother's bathroom transforms from a place of makeup and hairstyling tools: it's her church, she says, a realm where her awareness expands beyond the body she inhabits. A place where we can't touch her.

6.

Dying from a broken heart is rare, but can happen: it's called broken heart syndrome. Happiness is 50 percent genetic. A baby's cells continue living inside her mother's brain. Of all parent-child relationships, science shows that mother-daughter bonds are the strongest. 36 percent of Americans say the form of immortality they'd choose is to be remembered by history.

Forget the body's calamities, the ways it breaks: instead, I picture Frances swimming off Venice Beach in her early twenties, the simple years, carefree and worryless, drifting on her back far from the spot where her bright towel and Budweiser wait in the sand, her eyes closed to the sun as she imagines the fun she'll find that night. Forget the body's grief: after my parents' divorce, my mom starts hiking for the first time in her life, traveling through thick Appalachian woods and high Sierra trails, sore and exhausted to the point of tears, her body a combustion engine. One night, she backpacks to the bottom of Bryce Canyon to camp beneath red spires, the furthest she's ever slept from the rest of the world, she says, her physical strength and anger having carried her into her new life. Forget the ways we forget the body: my sister Mallory wakes each day at four a.m. to lift weights, flip tires, perform pull-ups and push-ups, run outside through the crisp desert morning, finding pennies in the road, veering onto sagebrush trails, dodging rocks and holes and occasional snakes, her body carving new muscle from devotion to itself. Forget the body's limits: my sister-in-law Randie trains for the Ironman Triathlon after her second baby is born. For two years, she keeps a handwritten training schedule and maintains strict discipline before she flies to Texas to swim 2½ miles, bicycle for 112 more, then run a 26-mile marathon. We watch on our laptops, tracking her bib number throughout the day and into the night when the runners seem to travel largely solo. We have tears in our eyes when we watch her cross the finish line in the dark, a smile of relief on her face, so many months culminating in this moment.

To recognize the wonder after all this time: when I coached, I'd spot the girls as they repeated drills on the bars and mats, some with their blisters taped and ankles wrapped, the falls or sprains no match for their willingness to try again the risky skill or difficult sequence. I couldn't see it then, but joy eclipsed their pain. And to think I'd stood below them, my own heart racing as I watched.

TRANSCRIPT: VINYL

ASHLEY FARMER: How long did you work at Capitol Records?

FRANCES DRESSER: Off and on, through the years. I can't tell you an exact time. Because I used to quit or come in late on Mondays—every other Monday [*laughs*]. But I worked there for quite a while. My sister Della worked there the longest.

AF: Can you remember certain records that you pressed?

FD: A lot of Nat King Cole.

AF: Really? I love Nat King Cole.

FD: I do, too.

MINIVAN, 1994

We gas the family minivan, Brendan and I, light out to literal
greener pastures with my new driver's license, Oldham County
to Henry County, a tinge of spring among the horses and silos. The
Kinks sing about a sunny afternoon, a Waterloo sunset, a dead-end
street. In Buckner, the stoplight sits beside the taxidermy shop.
If your car pauses in that spot, you might watch men's hands
move across some unseen animal. I have dollars from my job at the
video store but nowhere to go. My brother plays deejay with the
CDs. The Mamas and the Papas. The Beach Boys, the Zombies.
I taste Dr Pepper lip balm mixed with a clove cigarette on my
lips. The thin highway rolls, the edge and its ditch always close:
my mother swears kids never crashed so much when she was our
age in Long Beach but here it's easy to speed, to slide over the
white line and drift into redbuds. We play Neil Young and the
Dead. Van Morrison's *Astral Weeks*. We long for my parents' era,
years filtered through a warm lens, tinged with goldenrod, with
weed and psychedelia, soaked in salty sea. We want to live inside
a time that isn't this one. Things will erupt soon, my mom and dad
busted apart, the house gone, our nucleus unglued. Sweet, maybe,
how my brother gave me Mace, a spray can in a leather holster,
just in case, he said. His friend had a gun once, but he swears it's
buried in the woods. We sing to "Sweet Thing," though we don't
know the blue ocean and can't see tomorrow's sky. We roll the
windows down, though the chill cuts through our sweaters and
burns our cheeks.

TRANSCRIPT: BEACHES

BILL DRESSER: I liked Venice best.

ASHLEY FARMER: Why did you like Venice best?

BD: Well, the beach.

FRANCES DRESSER: Why didn't we move there then? Why did we move to Long Beach?

BD: Well, Frances . . .

FD: We never considered moving to Venice.

BD: I'm talking about when I was a kid.

AF: You probably remember Long Beach when there were waves there?

BD: Waves?

AF: There are no waves in Long Beach now.

FD: There isn't?

AF: No, because of breakwaters. So it's all still. What were some places you and Grandpa used to go when you were dating?

FD: We went to Sunset Beach and different beaches. What did we used to do before we got married? And don't tell everything!

BD: Ha! Go to the beach. We'd get some tomatoes and—

FD: Dill pickles.

BD: Yep. And a couple of brewskis.

AF: What was your favorite beach?

BD: Well, after we got married, it was Redondo or Huntington Beach.

AF: Grandpa, do you remember when there were waves in Long Beach?

BD: There were good waves. In fact, that's where surfboards first originated.

AF: Really?

BD: Yeah, our lifeguard—his name was Cox—and he was from Hawaii and he became a lifeguard in Venice. And we had delinquent kids and he decided to kinda get them straightened out. And he had developed the VPC, Venice Paddleboard Club— they didn't call them surfboards then or whatever they call them now—and for five dollars (which I was never able to get together) you could make your own surfboard. It was plywood, hollow. Back then that was what they used. And they didn't develop the real surfboards—oh, the first ones they did were made out of laminated balsa and redwood. They weighed about a ton and you had to be a kind of hefty person to handle one of them. Then they made them smaller and smaller. But they had real good waves at Venice. I never got into surfboarding because I never really had the opportunity. But I used to bodysurf—you could catch a wave with bodysurfing.

AF: Could you see the ocean from your house?

BD: She could see Catalina Island!

FD: On top of where I lived, if it was a clear day.

AF: I can see it from where I teach, if it's clear.

BD: I wonder if that old ship is still stuck out there.

AF: What ship?

BD: That ship that sunk out there off of Palos Verdes. Remember, we took a ride one time—I played hooky from work and we—

FD: Oh, yeah—

BD: Yeah, I think divers and stuff had surrounded it. It hit on the rocks and didn't sink all the way so you could still see part of it.

BILL, 1925–2016

He meets Frances at the Blue Bird Bar on her birthday afternoon when she isn't twenty-one yet. I picture flecks of light through a dive's dark windows. Among things I wish I'd asked him: what he sensed when he saw her, what they drank, how he asked for her number. On an early date, she gets so furious at him that she kicks in the door of his car. "See you around," I can hear her say before she travels to the desert without him (she returns, of course, gardenias in her bra and hair). They party, swim. She watches him do iron crosses and handstands at Muscle Beach. They crash a car and he laughs when he tells me how it flipped and sailed, nobody injured. They fashion a life, much of it made from his hands: the shipyard living, the boats and furniture, his rows of Russian olive trees, the jewelry with polished turquoise stones at their centers. When I'm little, I sidekick in his orange Willys Jeep and he squeezes my hand, rolls it in a way that almost hurts, like how you long to crush a thing you love. In this family of talkers, drinkers, weepers, guitar players, he's more reserved, a planner. When he comes home from jail, my mother never asks whether he and Frances discussed the gun. Instead, my mother makes him swear to stay alive. He says he will, but still, she finds a rope in the shed he built. Another time, she finds him in the car in the garage with the engine running, though he says it's nothing and plays it off. If you asked me if I knew him well, I would say yes. Yet how to reconcile that he took someone's life? I'll fail forever at this. Before he died, he swore it was the greatest thing he ever did.

SEEING THE DEAD ALIVE

We ditched California, Ryan and I, crossed the Kentucky state line. Then the art museum called: I'd applied as an educator. I bought a blazer on deep discount and rearranged myself for a series of interviews. I had some relevant experience but no art history degree—a visitor peeking through stained-glass windows. But the museum said yes.

My first week, I took a blurry selfie at the loading dock. There it is, my 2014 face, a spook in me because I still wore grief beneath my makeup, frayed and haywire and braced for the next bad thing.

Once you notice mortality inside the art museum, it comes into startling focus: oil paintings of political assassinations and burials at sea and long-gone wealthy couples with their serious children. Handmade mounts inside casework cradle the dead's jewelry and ceramics. Ornate dressers and chests rest on pedestals, furniture that once held the dead's laundry and letters. The artists who created these pieces? Gone.

My family isn't afraid of death.

But how to actually make sense of it? I longed to grieve my grandmother in a normal way, but normal had vanished and we had no time for the past, for missing her, for recalling how she sang to Sarah Vaughan or camped at alpine lakes to catch her limit or how she'd once transformed her spare bedroom into a painting studio, the scent of linseed oil wafting from under the door. We couldn't pause for grief and we couldn't process my grandfather's crime because we waited for the law to do it.

My grandmother's life doesn't equal her death. Yet I keep writing and rewriting her ending because I learned from her suffering that you can die more than once: your life can leave you, but you can still die further, a more final death. The inverse is true, too: you can find yourself paused just outside of death like my grandfather, who'd chosen to end his life but found himself accidentally alive, walking his desert yard while out on parole, reading the newspaper in his pale blue chair, drinking coffee in the sun with my mom while he waited for the law to decide what remained of him.

\/◂

I didn't think of myself as an artist, an art person. Most of what I knew about art came from a college art history course and some figure-drawing classes. In graduate school, I enrolled in studio art for nonmajors and spent multiple class sessions painting a tabletop birthday party scene the instructor had assembled. Over time, the pink grocery store cake refused to rot and I kept at it, slicking more paint, the pink icing on my canvas growing thicker, and the instructor calling my style aggressive—something that maybe wasn't a compliment but that I liked anyhow.

As I trudged home through shin-deep snow, art portfolio in one freezing hand, phone in the other, I'd sometimes call my mom or grandmother, a three-hour time difference separating my upstate New York life and theirs in Nevada with my grandfather. Both women were legitimate artists who'd gifted me more landscapes and birds and abstract works than I could hang in my tiny apartment: I had to rotate their pieces, storing extras next to sweaters in my closet. I hadn't inherited their talent, but I'd learned to love the act of making, how time paused in the studio, the instructor's music playing, the sugary pink cake still standing, the party never over, my family tucked away and safe on their sun-soaked desert hill.

\/.

I didn't think of myself as an art person because I thought of myself as an English person, a writing person. But adjunct teaching had shaved me down. Those first days back in Kentucky, I saw a doctor for sleep, a man with wildlife photos on his walls. I applied for job after job and ran the perimeter of the small-plane airport in my neon pink shoes until I wore holes in the toes. On my first day at the art museum, they showed me my office chair, my desk with a computer, the pen holder and stapler. Nothing special, any of it, but I could hardly believe my luck: the steadiness these objects represented. The ordinary beauty and relief.

\/.

The Speed Art Museum sits on my undergrad campus. One change: vinyl decals now ban weapons from university buildings. You'll find these stickers on the museum's doors, too. They tell visitors, "Maybe death lives in the art museum, but you can't bring death inside. This is a space for us to go on living."

\/.

Just before we skipped LA, my brother Brendan visited. He stepped off the plane midbender. Ryan and I hadn't anticipated this, how full-blown my sibling's condition had become. I Googled facilities—thirty days, sixty—even though none of us had money and he'd been not long ago to a place where they'd let him write songs on an upright piano. I wanted to transport him on a plane to someone who could cure him or to someplace safe, wherever that was, maybe the pale-yellow bedroom we'd shared as kids or the thin-walled city apartment on Speed Avenue that we'd shared in our twenties, back when things were still fun, when recklessness felt like a harmless, reversible choice.

It was bad, but he said he wouldn't drink for three days, that he could manage withdrawal without doctors, that he'd get help when he returned home. To bridge the gap, Ryan bought him the strongest weed imaginable from a neighbor, which helped some. Still, I didn't know how to kill our anxious time except to drive. We drove from Long Beach, above the harbor where my grand-father had worked, through Huntington Beach, where my mother had watched surfers with her girlfriends, up to Venice, where my grandparents spent their wild years. I rolled our windows down to a cloudless day, the blue and bougainvillea somehow bruising, making things painful, jets streaking the sky and my brother on a knife's edge. At the boardwalk, people rollerbladed past us, offered to read our palms. I wanted to call someone for help, but we were adults: Who was supposed to rescue us?

We ended up at the contemporary art museum where there was a special exhibition about skate art. My brother had skated as a teenager, spent whole weekends with his friend in the city near Bardstown Road where they could skate from morning until night. I didn't know most of the artists in this show, just Banksy and Stüssy, a guy who'd happened to go to high school with our mom. We stayed for hours, looked at every work—the neon graffiti, the elaborate murals and installations of 1970s New York subways—sometimes talking, sometimes not. I took pictures of us that I'll always wish I hadn't lost.

Driving home, I saw a young guy nodding off against a bright white stucco storefront. Blocks from there, I'd once visited the mural where someone had photographed Elliott Smith for his *Figure 8* album cover. My brother had given me news of Smith's death over the phone—we were both big fans. The wall is a swirl of red, white, and black and people had gathered there, lit clusters of candles against it. Someone handed me a Sharpie to add my condolences and this stranger, a drag queen made up for a performance, gave me a long hug. I didn't cry that day, but I could've now as I drove down Sunset at sunset with my brother, his face turned away from mine as the city turned on for the night, the Hollywood sign to my left, this iconic stretch a fresh canvas but also a familiar work. Dusk just before it got dark.

In one of the museum's galleries, there's a strange, sweet Chagall painting framed in gold, a primary-color landscape in which humans and animals float above a sleeping town. A few years before the museum hired me, my brother was still in Louisville and he'd worked with people recovering from brain injuries. His job was to accompany them to public places they enjoyed. For some, the art museum was one of these spots. After I'd gotten the museum job, he called me from Austin where he lived now in a sober house and he asked me if the Chagall was still up. I told him it was. This was a good stretch—I could hear it in his voice, the intense clarity, the desire to cover so much territory as we caught up. Our reciprocal happiness buzzed through the phone. "That was always my favorite," he said.

◣/◤

Sometimes people would call the museum to inquire about donating a painting they discovered in their uncle's barn or an inherited hutch with a faded foil on the back. "I want the museum to have it," they'd say. "Can you take it?" they'd ask. But it's not so simple: when museums take objects into their collections, they're committing to caring for those works of art in perpetuity. Can you imagine trying to save something precious forever?

◣/◤

I'm trying to save something precious forever.

◣/◤

When they released him from jail, my mom had to keep a careful eye on my grandfather. It was like holding on to glass. "You have to promise me you won't do anything," she pleaded when she picked him up late that night. "I couldn't take it." The jail psychiatrist had assessed him, deemed him safe to go home, and asked him outright if he would keep care of himself, if he would promise not to end his life. My grandfather agreed. Yet, every time he drove down the hill to the mailbox or every time my mom went into town to buy groceries, she worried.

When I'd visit, he and I talked like we always had, sometimes about my grandmother, sometimes not, and never about the shooting. We drank diet sodas in lawn chairs and watched lizards skitter on the deck. I'd kiss his cheek and tell him I loved him, even though he was shy about those words. I wasn't shy: straightforwardness about love felt urgent now. Meanwhile, my grandmother's paintings in the living room, the hallway, the bedrooms took on new significance. Details I hadn't noticed—the delicate spray of white sea foam or the smooth texture of cherries against a black background—emerged, each one reflecting the talent and skill she possessed, the hours of lessons she'd taken, her years of practice. A fleck of light on a vase seemed so deliberate. Forbidding skies and abandoned buildings in her landscapes resonated differently now. I could view her as an artist and see her works as something separate from all I thought I'd known about her.

My grandfather had lived the life of an artist in his own way, too: the boats he built, the houses he made, the wood carvings, all of it precise and disciplined, mathematical. He crafted furniture from willow branches for Brendan and me when we were little kids, matching child-sized chairs. The bed I sleep in when I visit my mom, a meticulous oak piece with dramatic flourishes: he'd made it for Frances.

✓◄

Conservators store photographs far from light, remove wax from bronze sculptures with a scientist's touch. Drawings are bathed, dried, and blotted. A delicate quilt might be displayed for a few short months before it's back to storage where it can rest for years. Special flecked windows reflect the sun.

When my bones become dust in the sagebrush near my grand-mother's, these works that existed for centuries before me will likely continue to tell their stories.

✓◄

I was at my desk in the black chair when my mom called. It was the middle of the day, so she knew I was at work. In my mind, this meant fresh tragedy: I now dreaded calls at odd times or from numbers I didn't recognize. I knew to step outside before calling her back.

"It's all over," she said.

The district attorney had dismissed the case: he couldn't condone my grandfather's actions, but he couldn't find the malice in them either. In a lengthy piece of writing, the DA articulated all that was morally ambiguous about the shooting and weighed it against my grandfather's age and health issues—and, maybe most significantly, what his expensive treatments and prescriptions would cost the state if they incarcerated him. The DA had considered statements our family had written, which explained that we didn't want my grandfather prosecuted. The hospital didn't encourage punishment either. And ultimately, he'd read multiple accounts of my grandmother's words: "I want to die," more than once, in different, yet unambiguous, phrasings. My grandfather had committed a crime, but it was victimless, they said, so he wouldn't go to prison. I hung up and cried into my hands as I hid my face against the window of the next-door restaurant that hadn't yet opened for dinner, its chairs inside resting on top of the dark wood tables.

✓

In 2016, my grandfather died in the home he built with his hands. Our family's artwork hung on the walls around him: a train my mom painted to his left and one of my grandmother's seascapes—the Pacific crashing on rocks—likely the last thing he saw.

✓

On my dresser, Cameron's ceramic bowls cradle tangles of necklaces. In any given room I might find his vases or cups or small, curved dishes glazed in earth tones. In middle school, he won an award that let him study art on the weekends in the next county over, painting and drawing on Saturday mornings. When he received a full ride to college for engineering, he did well in his subject but ended up trading it for an art major. Today, his metal sculptures adorn family members' yards and the redwood bench he crafted sits beneath our grandfather's now-tall olive trees.

Mallory's watercolors hang on my wall and lean against the lamp on my dresser—golden aspens with ivory trunks, a clutch of lush spring flowers or a vase of daisies, each artwork reflecting her skill and delicate touch.

On my phone, photos of sketches Brendan made in ink or bright pencil, images he's emailed or texted me without a word.

These are the artifacts, the evidence of who they are and were.

\/◄

I'm not the artist my family members are, but I write. When I write, I'm trying to make something like the cake in the studio, an observation of what once was. I'm trying to build a house.

Ryan writes, too. When I told him I've been writing about 2014, he cautioned me: "Those were dark days. You have to let in a little light." Because what's darkness without contrast? That's good advice, the light.

\/◄

We went to a different art museum recently, the Art Institute of Chicago, as the city bustled with holiday tourists. I'd visited this museum once long ago, but now it stunned me. When we encountered Marc Chagall's *America Windows*, it was by accident, these illuminated panels of primary-colored stained glass over thirty feet in length, breathtaking scenes depicting various art forms while figures float in a cobalt sky and a moon pierces through shades of blue. I stood in silence next to reverent strangers. The dreamlike scene felt so familiar to me, I could've stepped inside that work of art. Lived there for a little while.

Ryan and I lingered in the galleries until lights dimmed to signal closing and then we straggled outside with other visitors bundled in coats—some who, like us, hauled their luggage down the massive steps because they'd come straight from the airport, the art museum their first stop in the city. We waited for our ride in the dark. Overwhelm swelled in my chest at the thought that what we make may outlast us. What I'd seen that day: it could sustain me for a very long time.

TRANSCRIPT: GAMES

BILL DRESSER: When we were kids, it was so much different than it is nowadays. We had games like kick the can and hide-and-go-seek and alley, alley over—you'd throw the ball over the top of your house and someone on the other side would catch it and throw it back. And we'd make our own toys. About the only toys we ever got were maybe roller skates or a wagon. But I think nowadays kids get all this stuff and they never try to improvise anything. We used to make stilts—you know what they are?

FRANCES DRESSER: You made those for the kids.

BD: And if you'd get a pair of old roller skates, you used to make a skate-coaster. There were a lot of games we used to play. What was that other one where you'd grab a prisoner and put him in . . . ?

FD: But they might even still do that, I don't know.

BD: And hopscotch.

ASHLEY FARMER: You had a lot more freedom, too, didn't you?

BD: Yeah. My parents didn't worry too much about us [laughs]. You could tell, Carthay Circle, that was a big deal and they got enough money together and we were able to go, but we rode the streetcar there.

FD: Saw special movies that were coming out . . .

AF: So, your [Frances's] parents were kind of strict?

FD: Real strict.

BD: We—my sister, my mom, myself—we'd walk to the beach. It was a pretty good walk from where we lived.

AF: Do you know what street you lived on?

BD: Yeah, Tivoli Avenue. It was just a short walk to Venice High School. In fact, our street ran into the high school. My mother, my sister, and I would walk to the beach. And back in those days, people didn't think about littering. It was just an accepted thing. You'd drink a soda and throw it out the window. So we'd walk along and pick up these bottles. And then when we got to the beach, my mom would take them in and get the deposits and then we'd buy candy.

AF: That's cool.

BD: You could get a candy bar for a nickel or you could get a tamale for a nickel. And I'd get a tamale and then think, "Damn, I wish I would've got a candy bar." [Laughs.] This was the Depression, you know.

FD: Even when Vic was a kid, he says, "Mom, can I take those beer bottles down to the liquor store and get the refund?" And I go, "Oh, okay. Go ahead." And the bottles were a nickel. And he came back and I says, "What happened?" and the guy had said you can't get the refund here—we don't do it.

So, I just hopped in the car and went down there. I said, "Look, we buy all our beer here and when he comes down for the deposit I expect him to get it. And I'll send him on down as soon as we buy it." I was about to kill him! [*Laughs.*]

BD: And another thing: we used to live in another place (we moved around a lot). This particular street was in Los Angeles, Carmona Avenue. And they had this big hill and in the cement they put 57—this advertising for Heinz 57. And we'd go up there and get a cardboard and we'd get on the top of that big ol' thing and slide down the Heinz 57 [*laughs*]. And we'd get a pretty good ride, you know! Then we'd hike back up there, on that cardboard and *shooooooo*! That's some of the fun things we used to do.

AF: That's scary. That's awesome [*laughs*].

BD: And I might have told you this experience I had: one time I decided to make myself a surfboard and I got some boxes and wood and stuff and put it together and painted it. I remember that I painted a little airplane on it. Little black paint. I painted the board blue and painted that airplane on her. Boy, I just couldn't wait to get down to the beach and every day I'd wait and that damn paint wasn't dry yet. I'd keep checking it. Finally I said, ah hell, I'm going to go anyway. I went down there with that surfboard and it was just like sandpaper. The sand stuck to the paint [*laughs*]. But eventually I made a pretty good surfboard.

FOUR

TRANSCRIPT: MATRIMONY

FRANCES DRESSER: Do you know how long we've been married?

ASHLEY FARMER: How long?

FD: Sixty-two years.

BILL DRESSER: Sixty-THREE years.

FD: Let's get this, right. Let's see, how old is Vic? [*Laughs.*]

AF: Sixty-three! That's pretty good. You know each other pretty well by now.

BD: Pretty much.

FD: Pretty damn well. But not everything!

AF: Not everything. That's good.

BD: She's still got secrets?

FD: You know me—old blabbermouth. Geez, it blows me away to say we've been married sixty-three years. Never regretted it. Maybe once or twice [*laughs*].

THE BOOK I WOULD'VE
WRITTEN WITH NO
TROUBLE IN IT

My teenage mom goes to an art show with Frances. There's a contest for amateurs, the judge a famous seascape artist my grandmother admires. Before they drive there, my mom sneaks one of Frances's paintings into the car. When the organizer calls for entries, my mom submits her mother's work. Frances is surprised, but glad: she never would've entered, and definitely not with a seascape to be judged by the seascape expert. "What is that?" my grandmother whispers to my mom when they announce the winners. It's a blue ribbon on her frame.

◄╱◄

My parents collide in love at Club Continental Apartments. 1976. Young, lean years. My mom with her shag, my dad with his Peter Frampton perm. They swim at the beach, soak in the apartment complex hot tub. The first time he proposes it's from beneath a car he's fixing and she pretends not to hear him. Her bridesmaids wear mint-green dresses and crowns of flowers. Family and friends attend, a cast of characters: the dance troupe led by a guy named Ace, the topless skier now dating a celebrity golfer, a neighbor who wears a towel on her head and tells people at the reception they're going "straight up," as in, maybe, to heaven.

\/◄

My mom is twenty-four when I arrive. Frances, who has just moved to Nevada, returns to California for my birth. I show up at St. Joseph's in Orange where they have a contest for the one hundred thousandth baby born. I'm only hours off from winning the prize.

\/◄

High desert, mountains, alpine lakes, dirt, no shirt, my aunt's quarter horses, the chickens, sprinklers, and popsicles from frozen juice. A shopping cart in the sand dune like a UFO. I make tea plant tents with boys who live down the road.

My mom's little sister Kelly buys me stickers, puffy and scratch-and-sniff and Lisa Frank. She drives me to the lake and the hot springs, takes me Christmas caroling on the back of her horse, Genoa, who wears bells on his ankles. On that same horse, she gives rides to kids at my backyard birthday party when I'm five. She dances at a park celebration and I'm mesmerized by her tap shoes, her glitter, her top hat and cane. She has a white dog named Zeppelin. She writes songs on an acoustic guitar and I love the lyrics to one about a breakup in which the singer refuses to cry.

\/◄

I break my arm in a backyard fall, another time on the Slip 'N Slide. Each injury means a milkshake after leaving the doctor. Soccer games give me occasional shiners because I'm tall and the tops of kids' heads line up with my eyes. But I like being on a team for the Gatorade and orange slices and saying *good game* as I high-five strangers.

✦✦✦

We move to Northern California where the golden hills look like shaggy animals. It's for my dad's job. A huge green electrical box sits in our yard, a spot like a pedestal where I read the Baby-Sitters Club books, Christopher Pike, *Anne of Green Gables*. Up there, next to my best friend, I imagine myself the star of the neighborhood. After my mom's last piano student leaves our house at dusk, she sits on the box instead with the neighbor who looks like Jackie Kennedy. They each drink a Bartles and Jaymes in the suburban sunset while kids shriek and run around the yard.

✦✦✦

On a Saturday morning, my brothers and I pile into my parents' bed: what's ours is theirs. My dad in his briefs, my mom in a powder-blue nightgown. We're a solid, unbreakable thing.

✦✦✦

My family drives to Folsom Lake with a picnic of fried chicken and potato salad. We fly flimsy rainbow kites from the grocery store. Boats on the water look like sharp, white birds. We sing to the radio on the way home and negotiate space with our siblings in the back seats. Brendan asks my dad to turn the radio up. Mallory, a toddler, falls asleep in her car seat while Cam leans his head against my arm, his face warm with sun.

✦✦✦

We move to Kentucky for my dad's job when I'm thirteen. Where's Kentucky? We unpack boxes in hobbling heat and humidity. A neighbor kid wanders over, walks through our front door, and says, "Why don't you turn on your air conditioning?" We didn't know we had air conditioning.

\/◂

The stories we retell about one another, the siblings. How Cameron notes that the broken trees in our new town are from a tornado that arrived before us, so this little boy who eventually becomes a fire-fighter prepares a basement safety kit with water, flashlights, a radio. How in high school he plays Oberon beneath green stage lights and gives speeches to the student body as their president. How Mallory and I play the car game on our Highway 22 porch: the ones headed east are hers, the westbound ones mine, and we imagine where we'll drive. How she adjusts my makeup and suggests different clothes before I go out even though I'm the teenager and she's a kid. How Brendan practices the same skateboard trick again and again or the time he quietly gives his prized sneakers away to someone at school who needed shoes. The narratives we repeat in an attempt to sum up people we love and, therefore, can't.

\/◂

In middle and high school, I visit Bill and Frances for chunks of summer. I lose frequently at backgammon and rarely at Boggle and always at cribbage. I discover her Richard Brautigan books, Tom Robbins. Frances has a dictionary in which she marks any word she looks up. The pages are sprinkled with checkmarks.

\/◂

Frances writes me letters in looping, precise cursive. She sticks sprigs of sagebrush inside so I don't forget how it smells.

PIANO HOUR, 1995

Homecoming comes and goes. So does the black velvet dress I wear beneath stadium lights, same as another girl's, a designer knockoff inspired by a Demi Moore movie. We're coatless and goose-bumped and giddy in the cold as the marching band warms up. We're grown enough, not grown. Cornstalks bend at angles I should know from geometry class. At the piano bench each night, the timer can't end my practice fast enough. I don't study music the way I don't study math: instead, I press the keys and think about my crush's heavy lashes, the loose-leaf poems in my backpack, which sweater I'll wear tomorrow so that I stand a chance of standing out against the forest of dark-green lockers where students kiss and cry. Tonight, I'll call my best friend, Katie, at exactly eleven when she'll dial the weather line and wait for me, our trick for guaranteeing our parents won't hear the phone ring. Pachelbel's Canon in D is all repetition and dynamics, crescendo and diminuendo—another trick. Brick house, broken corn, football lights, a song that lasts too long: the woman's voice on the time and temperature line never changes. *We're here*, she says, *and it'll frost tonight, but you can find music in anything.*

END OF THE LINE

1.

For my sixteenth birthday, my mom brought me to a psychic. A fun thing, we figured, as we drove to the woman's house that spring morning. Would she mention overseas adventures or a Broadway stint? Would I fall in love with a beach town local like in romance novels I'd grown up reading? I felt giddy and greedy to know my destiny. But the psychic's predictions weren't what I'd wished. "You'll write and you'll teach," she said. "You'll marry twice. And I see twin boys."

We kept a recording from that day, one I've returned to since: the psychic was mostly right about jobs and joy and relationships. But the twins never materialized, and I suppose I've waited for them all these years, their matching faces side by side within a locket.

When I met Ryan, we became serious fast: new love means making up for lost time. We stayed up beyond late each night, relaying every detail of our lives before heading to work, dizzy and infatuated. I slept so little that my right eye twitched for a month.

One night, ambulance lights flashed and we sat up in bed to find paramedics at his neighbors' front door. We knew it was grave from the crew's slow pace and the absence of sirens and the unhurried cop, and we kept vigil, not gawking, just waiting, minutes spinning into hours because we felt compelled to see through to the end whatever had happened.

We made future plans together in that dark part of morning,

imagining a life together. Regarding kids, which I told him I wanted one day, Ryan agreed, "That's just what you do." His conviction impressed me, the fact that he could settle on something so forever without heavy introspection or at least a pro/con list. It felt like a psychic leveling a prediction.

2.

When my parents married near the ocean, you could see Disneyland from their apartment complex, a place for hippies and surfers and young Vietnam veterans and community college students and ex-cons and also current cons, like the guy on the lam who taught tennis lessons under an alias. My mom saw a doctor when she thought she might be pregnant. The lab results said she wasn't. She'd felt so certain and now this news crushed her and my dad held her as she cried. Later on, he told me they hadn't planned for kids yet—hadn't planned for anything—but after seeing her so distraught, he suddenly hoped for a baby.

"I just knew I was pregnant," my mom said. She'd been right all along and it was me.

Up the freeway in Eagle Rock, five decades before my arrival, my great-grandmother gave birth for the seventh of what would be nine times.

"It's a girl! Just like you wanted!" the doctor said when he delivered my grandmother, Frances.

"Who said I wanted another kid?" my great-grandmother replied.

It's a funny anecdote in our family, but when Frances told it, she expressed empathy beneath the joke, an understanding for her mother who was overworked and married to a difficult man in a difficult era. "She was so smart," Frances would say and explain how her mother loved poetry—how that, even with nine kids in the middle of the Great Depression, there was so much more to her mother than motherhood.

As a child, I didn't dream of being a mother, but I wanted to be *my* mother, or the paper doll version of her, cute and content and wide-smiling with babies in my lap as I sat on a back porch at dusk. Portulaca, paintings, impromptu road trips, anonymous gifts to strangers: my mother made brightness materialize. How lucky for us to sit at the center of her life.

And it was fun, she swears, the homemade Halloween parties and camping trips and the old cargo van filled with us plus neighbor kids for long lake days, her plastic beach chair at the water's edge. It was fun, she says, being the parent my own friends could confide in, the mom who hosted high school theater sleepovers and my brothers' rock bands in the basement, who invited our friends with difficult circumstances to move in for stretches, sometimes months or even years, making up the spare bed with clean sheets and stocking extra boxes of frozen waffles.

She wasn't just my mother, but a mother at the cellular level. "I was meant to be a mom," she says. "That's what I came to Earth to do."

3.

When I was nine, Santa brought me an electric typewriter for Christmas. *So long, babies,* I thought as I abandoned my dolls on the bed to instead write sentences on paper that jammed and bunched inside the gears. In my bedroom where we played after school, my friends tucked blankets around Cabbage Patch Kids, tipped plastic bottles with disappearing milk to the dolls' lips. But I wasn't satisfied with the same thing now: instead, I loved the mechanics of the typewriter, how grown-up it felt to sit in a chair that way, to see words and sentences materialize in front of me, no matter how simple. My friends and I reached a compromise: instead of playing house, we'd play *Annie*, a movie we'd just discovered from an earlier era and now loved. My friends would take care of kids in the orphanage, and I'd be the character who didn't exist, someone in the office keeping records or a reporter writing a story—anything to click the keys.

✓╱◄

Ryan and I had just married when I attended a poolside bridal shower in Los Angeles and sipped prosecco in a cabana. Feeling out of place but buoyant, I toasted with mostly strangers: I knew the bride and one other woman, the hostess who was also a writer I greatly admire. Conversation bubbled, the group giddy in their spring party attire, everyone mooning over the bride's wedding ideas.

Talk shifted to babies. Sharing a photo of her infant, the woman beside me asked, "Do you have kids?"

"No, no kids for us," I said in the breezy tone I'd practiced with distant relatives and grocery clerks and guys at the oil change place who'd once wondered aloud where my children were.

"But you want them, right?" she asked. I felt warmth in my cheeks.

"I'm not sure," I said, which was the truth. The woman seemed bewildered, as though she hadn't accounted for this, meeting someone who felt ambivalent about motherhood, and awkwardness hung in the air, souring the ladies-at-a-fancy-party vibe.

But the hostess interrupted. "Not every woman has to have kids. Not every woman needs to be a mother."

After all, she wasn't a mother. How many brunch moments like this had she experienced?

Years later, I recall the details—bright sundresses, miniature French-soap party favors, the summer scent of chlorine from the pool that I wanted to dive into—and how those two sentences, delivered with no apology, issued me permission.

The Gulf of Mexico washed gobs of tar from BP's Deepwater Horizon oil spill onto the shore where I sat in beach chairs with Ryan and his mom after a day of drinks and swimming and reading books on a family vacation. That's when the topic arose, when we'd have kids. So much time had passed, so many conversations. Through them, Ryan had revised his idea that having kids is "just what you do" and, for the both of us, it felt less clear-cut than ever—almost a surprise that maybe we were lucky enough with the life we had, just the two of us. And perhaps we tossed the words out too casually, the heat and the strange ecological disaster distracting us from taking a softer tack, but we said we weren't sure. His mother teared up, a reaction that took us by surprise, something we hadn't expected. She hadn't expected this, either. This woman I adore, who has always treated me like one of her own, would never pressure us, of course. But life for her, she said, hadn't really started until she became a mother.

My mom and I had lunch at a brewery a few months after Frances died. John Lennon sang "Come Together" over the speakers: Frances loved the Beatles and we took it as some sort of sign. Why not? We were tired—my mom especially, after all that had happened—and I picked at salty fries as we sat at a sunny window table and talked about our family lineage, about substance abuse and mental health, so many fractured branches of our family tree. I told her I didn't think kids were in the cards for me.

She seemed unfazed, but what could faze her now?

"You could always change your mind someday?" It was non-chalance meant as acceptance and I felt relief as the waiter set the check on the table.

Isn't it enough that I had a childhood once? Sat in the car wash with my father, pink foam swirling on the windshield, grape gum in my mouth and Prince on the radio, both of us singing our hearts out? That I followed my mother around the desert yard at dusk in awe of her magic as she doused the saplings? Curled up on the floral sofa with my brothers to watch bad '90s sitcoms on week-nights after homework? Peeked in to see my little sister sleeping as *Cinderella* played on her miniature television every night for three years? Happiness and luck, my parents even in love once, and I was there. Why should I try to recreate it?

\/

Last year, Ryan's dad, John, became confused as he left a Louisville Cardinals basketball game. At home, he spread mail across the kitchen in a peculiar way, left baseball caps organized in odd places. Ryan's brother drove him to the doctor where they delivered the terrible news that undiagnosed lung cancer had metastasized in John's brain. He was already near the end before he knew what had begun.

Two months later, as we celebrated the holidays under their roof and John grew weaker, every tradition—Christmas Eve egg rolls, the lottery scratch-offs from the gas station, the find-the-pickle-ornament-in-the-tree game—carried the heft of being the last of its kind. Still, the adults rallied, baking sugar cookies and hyping Santa's arrival for our two young nieces. One evening, as we watched the "Baby Shark" video on repeat, the girls sprawled across our laps on the guest room bed, Ryan and I exchanged looks like *Maybe we could do this?*

John passed away that February. As the family planned funeral details like the bagpiper and readings and music, Ryan and I discussed parenthood with sudden urgency.

"When we get home, let's do it," Ryan said as we failed at falling asleep one night.

The subject reappeared across the sad trip in silent glances: as we stood in the funeral home with all of our friends, some of them now parents, and as Ryan moved John's no-longer-needed medical supplies to the basement near his own childhood Star Wars figurines. Sometimes, when we played toddler board games or cradled the dozing baby while extended family arranged sandwiches in the dining room, we'd hold each other's eyes. Maybe we'd missed the point of life all along.

◣╱◢

The Truckee River that runs through Reno freezes in the winter. When my brother Brendan's birthday passes and none of us can reach him, a slow worry swells in a way that is both familiar and new. I won't tell his story, but mine is helplessness. I send another Facebook message, my tether to him, and the checkmark reveals that he hasn't read any. Each note I send grows more urgent, though I'm trying to keep it cool, not freak out: *How's it going? What are you up to? Are you there? Let me know you're okay?*

Reno police find a man's body in the water. When I read about it in the paper, I learn that the person had no ID. The last time I talked to my brother, he'd lost his driver's license and needed a new one. There are other clues, too. Our family gathers on a text thread, even my divorced parents who aren't in touch, all of us asking questions, communicating logistics, wondering who, exactly, was the last person in contact with him and when. Panic surges beneath the factual surface of our messages: one of us will call hospitals, another will file a missing person report.

My brother was supposed to be born on our grandfather's birthday. My mom had to be induced and she could choose a day within a late January range. When she scheduled it, though, she misremembered her dad's birthdate by a day, but by the time she realized it, she couldn't change her appointment at the hospital—something we've laughed at over the years when my brother and grandfather blew out birthday candles one day apart, two separate cakes.

We find him finally, in a place we'd overlooked and further away, all of us elated and relieved to know he's okay, that this will mean help and safety. Goodbye, we say on the thread to one another. My coffee sits cold on the table.

A few days later, though, the shock of it catches me as I drive to work, a surprise: my body freezes as I hold the steering wheel on a familiar neighborhood street with its quiet park and empty ball field. It's like I've fallen through ice myself and can't catch my breath as I pull into the lot at work, gather my lunch and water bottle and bag, click the car lock on the key chain.

I think of our mother. How a child becomes an adult, but you're still a parent. You're still tethered to him when he's drowning, when he drowns.

4.

If the twins had shown up, what stories would I tell? Instead, this is a nonstory. *Once upon a time, a woman didn't do something and she went on not doing it, the end.* Is that a story at all? Yet it's one story of my life.

One story, one possibility. Yet I can nearly picture her, the other version of me—the mother version of me—sitting not at the bridal shower table near the blue pool but at the shallow end instead as her twin boys splash. That other version? Just like me, she can't fully envision a life more complete than the one she has— can't glimpse that reality, though she senses it there, a different universe she almost inhabited. It's impossible to imagine the other joy that could've been. But the world might always ask us to try.

GREEN GIRLS, 1996

Us lush-like in the green. Flesh and bone in thickets and cutoffs and my scarred shin the way Kentucky taught us. Katie drives and I ride passenger side in her white sedan so bygone that she'd sat in the same back seat as a kid. We park above the stoner-green hills with her Marlboro Lights, waiting an entire year for that one song to arrive on the radio. *Come home,* our mothers call from their bathtubs. *Back before ten,* they insist from their kitchens. But we're wholesome enough, that's the thing: leaves quiver above us like astrology scrolls from the IGA checkout line or the locker combination that drifts from my fist on loose-leaf that used to be living, breathing. When I met her on the sunset soccer field, thirteen, same team, both of us defense in neon-green jerseys, we picked dandelions near the goalposts and talked about rock bands as our forwards scored in the distance. Every girl, we're getting to the point of it. Like my other girlfriend's pristine version of "Blackbird" in the branches where sun lights up strangers' booze bottles and empty silver whip-its. Her guitar in the woods, no note missed: What more do you want from us? At Cherokee Park, we girls carry our mothers' ancient blankets to claim our spots in the grass and lay back like they did, a ritual. Our eyes closed, necklaces roping our throats, we pluck blades of grass without wishing tipsy boys throwing Frisbees would shamble near us. Instead, we photograph one another. We journal and read Anaïs Nin. It's not a gold cross but I wear my mother's abalone shard from the Goodwill and my grandmother's bird's nest charm on a chain. They're heavy in a good way—I sleep in them. In my lime-green bedroom we light nag champa and draw on my walls with Sharpies beneath Christmas lights. Song lyrics, poems. Love letters in code. We play my dad's Marantz stereo from before I was born with the green glow inside the receiver. It's his oversized sweater I wear when we climb through the basement window, dragging our knees across damp grass toward some guys who smell like tobacco and Popov and their fathers' colognes. They have nothing to say: How are their mouths empty when us girls have plenty? We don't stay. There's not much you can choose, but if your best friend drives fast enough down Highway 42 you can hang your arm out the window and feel the river on your wrist, the trees and mist, green swirling around you, a spell. Necklace with a cheap two-dollar crystal, too, like, *Let this protect us*. When the clasp from the chain meets the charms on my chest, I make a wish. I'm not religious but, believe me, I believe in something.

TRANSCRIPT: RIPTIDES

ASHLEY FARMER: Where did you guys meet?

BILL DRESSER: You want to tell her?

FRANCES DRESSER: Blue Bird Bar.

AF: Was it in LA?

BD: It was on South Vermont Avenue. That was one of the main streets back then. The main streets were Main, Figueroa, Vermont. Those were the north and south streets if you were wanting to go to LA or down south. I was a mail carrier.

FD: But you were living in Harbor City.

AF: What's Harbor City?

BD: It's a little town down toward the harbor area. It was off Central Avenue, I think.

FD: To go to the beach—once Jo and I were like teenagers and could kinda take care of ourselves—we would have to take the yellow streetcar down to someplace on Broadway and transfer and take the red car all the way to the beach.

BD: That red car ran right past my high school.

FD: Venice?

BD: Venice High.

AF: What did you do at the beach? Because you loved to surf. You would surf and bodysurf.

FD: What did we do? We picked up boys [*laughs*].

AF: Suntan? You loved to swim.

FD: Uh-huh. Jo and I. I always got the blond guy and I didn't like blond guys—I liked brown-haired guys.

BD: One time, Russell and I (that's a buddy of mine)—they have big signs, you know, Riptides—we would go in on the south side of the beach and there was a string of buoys floating—you know what they are, with the rope?—that went right down the middle of the beach. And we'd be okay as long as we stayed on the south side of the beach. Because if the riptide would get us, we could grab that rope with the buoys.

Well, this one time Russell missed and he got caught in the riptide and it was taking him right into Venice Pier and he was going to go right into the pier. So he grabbed this piling and this piling had all these barnacles on it—you know, pilings that hold the pier up?—he's hugging onto that. Well, I got in the lifeguard boat and they picked me up and went after him.

I remember them saying they couldn't get in any closer and they tossed him a rope with a float on it and he had to grab that—if he'd missed it would've taken him back under the pier. He was in a precarious situation. When they pulled out, all those cuts—none of them were real serious but there was a lot of them and the blood was running out and he's standing up there and blood running down his chest [*laughs*].

FD: Was it you that said that Eagle Rock's a happening place?

AF: Yes, that whole area like Eagle Rock, Echo Park, Los Feliz.

FD: I went to Eagle Rock High School with Bob [*her brother*].

BD: Venice Beach used to be a happening place back before it was incorporated by Los Angeles. When it became incorporated they knocked off a lot of gambling and a lot of things they used to have. They had a dog-racing track there in Venice.

AF: Where did you guys first live when you got married?

BD: We lived in a little apartment on Van Nuys Avenue in Los Angeles.

IF

If my grandmother hadn't fallen that afternoon.

If she'd fallen a different way, just by an inch or two.

If my grandmother's spine had survived it. If surgeons could fix it.

If my family believed in religion. Feared it.

If death didn't exist as a backup plan.

If the doctors had delivered the bad news differently.

If my grandfather hadn't been present when they said, "No hope."

If we lived in another country.

(A country with different gun laws, right-to-die laws.)

If the pawnshop had been closed on Sunday.

If pawnshops didn't sell guns.

If pawnshops that sold guns asked questions.

If a waiting period gave my grandfather time to rethink this.

If the hospital had metal detectors.

(If we lived in a country that didn't need metal detectors.)

If a spring from the gun hadn't dislodged.

If the gun broke apart before he shot my grandmother.

If there hadn't been a correctional officer at the hospital that day.

If there'd been a different correctional officer at the hospital that day.

If my grandfather was a young man.

If my grandfather didn't look harmless. Easy to apprehend.

If my grandfather was perceived as more threatening than tragic.

If my grandfather didn't have money to get bailed out.

If the district attorney was a different district attorney.

If we were better about mental health.

If he had succeeded and they were both simply gone in that moment.

If anything else instead: another set of questions.

FIVE

SECOND PERSON

Your love story? You can write the beginning. You can write the beginning and the middle, but not the ending. You can write the early-beginning and the late-beginning and the early-middle and even the middle-middle—but never the ending. There's no end in sight, and besides, if you were at the end, you wouldn't think to tell it because you'd be living it instead. But the beginning and the middle: You can type it. Revise it. Go over it the way water shapes rock, smoothing its jagged edges, polishing it in the sun.

How people feel about second-person perspective depends on who it is. Some readers say it's tedious and some English teachers ban it from classrooms. Writers on Twitter say it's an amateur move, too limiting—a claim to which other writers respond with successful examples: *Here, here, here.* Scholars publish essays with columns and diagrams to illustrate the different variations of second person because not every *you* is the same *you*: some *yous* are meant to be the reader, while other *yous* are clearly a narrator talking about herself through a thin disguise. Regardless, there's always caution. Don't let it make your writing lazy. Don't let it get claustrophobic. Tread lightly.

But before second person, it's first person, all *I* and *me*. You're solo in a way that makes you pine for a *you*. You imagine this person as a jewel. You picture the gleaming facets: a nightstand stacked with books, the cracked, colorful spines beside a glass of overnight tap water with its cluster of tiny bubbles. You conjure another's eyes, how they flicker with light as this person steps in from the storm, snowflakes melting into a dark wool collar. The feel of the other's hip in your palm as you sleep, your chest against another's back: you can imagine that, too. Even the clutter doesn't bother you, like the socks tossed near the hamper or the moisturizer in the bathroom, its cap left off in a rush. Still, the person remains abstract like that one Rothko painting, a gradation of reds—raspberry to persimmon to plum—that put an embarrassing lump in your throat when you visited a museum with an old friend, a reaction you couldn't explain, except it's the same feeling that swells when you cradle your dozing infant niece or hear Nat King Cole's "O Holy Night" over grocery store speakers at Christmas. Wonder, maybe. In those moments, your body becomes an exclamation point.

When you fly from Nevada to Louisville to visit him on a windy day in your pale-yellow tank top, it's because he said, "I think we could have fun together." It seemed so breezy and light, playful like a dare. And you *were* up for it, up for arriving at his side just to see—to take the calculated risk, knowing that you'd regret *not* buying the discounted ticket with the long Phoenix layover more than you'd regret a five-day trip that fizzled or didn't amount to much. At the very least, you'd have a story to tell your best friend or a future love, evidence of some tiny spontaneous bone in your body.

He picks you up. You rumble around in the dark and he drives his red Isuzu Hombre, a little truck with crank windows and a stubborn stick shift, through Highlands side streets and Cherokee Park shortcuts. You still know this part of town so well, but he knows it better than you do. When you relax against the seat—or try to appear relaxed, at least—you aren't yet aware that this truck will become your truck, too, and that you'll memorize its glitches and quirks along Southern California freeways, or that it'll break down on a steep hill near Acton, California, causing your hearts to stutter, and, on a different summer road trip, that the A/C won't work in the Mojave and that you two, together for years by then, will laugh about it, speeding with the windows down. You can't guess that in this small cab with its weathered Kentucky state map and fat, black books of CDs you'll discuss love, music, writing, sex, marriage, God, puns, drinks, dogs, dinner plans, fears, ambitions, books, movies, politics, old friends, new friends, job prospects, job losses, parents, siblings, childhood, beauty, grief, mortality, how you've changed, how he's changed, too, as you morph across the years, faster than the truck can keep up. When, during that Louisville trip, you push the door open and step out on your first date to a concert his friends are playing at Headliners and the spring evening is so crisp that he offers you his black jacket in what feels like an organically kind gesture, you'd never know that you'd log years much like this moment, walking beside him as seasons, geographies, priorities flip like pages in a book. Because the beginning doesn't announce itself. You never think, *This is the start.*

But you can replay the beginning after the fact: the yellow tank, raw silk with beige flowers and minuscule cutouts along the neckline, a shirt you paid too much for at a Reno department store with your mom on your twenty-fifth birthday when you were mostly broke. But because you wore it that whole first summer you fell in love with him, it seems now like it paid for itself. The moment you hold hands as you walk toward the concert despite not having been in each other's physical presence much, you're already a team somehow, moving through the dark to the small venue, shoes crunching the parking lot gravel, and your fingers laced in that steadying, private way. He was so skinny taking

Adderall to finish school and you were skinny, too, from coffee and insomnia, working at a gym where you'd coach kids and teenagers all day, moving nonstop, plus the stress of a recent divorce and its attendant upheaval, and now the shivery thrill of this, whatever this was. Yes, when you picture the beginning, the two of you— his shoulder blades through the thin vintage cowboy shirt with mother-of-pearl buttons, your leather sandals with the short heel that you could still walk fast in—there it is, water smoothing rock, all the signs that you'd assemble a life together, even though, in that moment, you probably wondered if your hand was sweating and why you never paint your nails and if you should go back to his place later that night if he asked you to, and you hoped he would.

You replay that summer soundtrack, the sound of Louisville, of Pavement and the Silver Jews and Wax Fang and Built to Spill and the Mountain Goats and Spoon, you passenger side, bumming his fruit-punch nicotine gum. Or how you'd sit on his Baringer Avenue porch swing while cicadas chirped or how you lounged in friends' Germantown lawn chairs to share beers, Kentucky feeling more Kentucky than ever since you returned from the desert, which is to say green-on-green, lush and tipsy, drenched in honey-colored evening light that makes your day jobs seem incidental because, like the Ohio River, the future spills out in front of you, anything possible.

In the second person, in the editing and revision, you polish and shine up even the dumb, embarrassing times, like your most overblown argument in the beginning-beginning, those days when you were delirious for each other but also intense and disagreeable. The fight happened in front of a small art gallery, and it wasn't sparked by some substantial issue like trust or where the relationship was headed, but by the fact that you wanted to look in the window longer and he wanted to make it across the intersection before the light changed. You'd never been angrier about something so trivial and you're pretty sure your voices rose and that you both stayed mad for hours, maybe days, the fight a blaring sign of everything uncaring and oblivious about the other person, of how this must be a rebound on your part, a bad decision on his, and you were clearly incompatible so why not call it off now, cut your losses, move on? But as you revisit and revise, what comes into focus from that moment is the brick storefront and the windchimes tinkling in the open door and how it was an early fall day, it must've been, because you remember those yellow blade-shaped leaves blanketing the sidewalks and gutters, and it was chilly—which was maybe part of his hurry, come to think of it—and you wonder now about the glazed ceramic vases in the window, indigos and blood reds, whether they've survived fourteen years. So much can happen in that time.

Maybe because your love occurred in a headlong rush, it's hard to pin down the moment when so much I fell away. Maybe it was on that yellow tank top day or the first-date concert where you clinked glasses and said cheers beneath the bar lights. Or when, eighteen months later, he helped you relocate to Syracuse for grad school before heading west for his own program and you sat on the open moving truck's bumper outside your new apartment and cried because you didn't know if you could weather another change without failing. Or maybe it's when, after months apart, you materialize in California with an enormous black suitcase by your side and he picks you up at LAX and you spend that contented, bare-bones summer in his Irvine graduate student housing with its industrial carpet and the wetlands three stories below his bedroom window, subsisting on iced black tea and late night dinners and

walks beneath purple jacarandas. Or maybe it's when you move out
to California and live together for the first time: you buy champagne
and explore your new neighborhood beneath rows of swaying
palms before losing your clothes across the kitchen, the living room,
the bare bedroom with its box fan and naked bed, the place filled
with your belongings divided for the last time into yours and his.

"You need to let in a little light," he says about this book. This
is it, this essay, as best as you can tell. But what's the brightness
without shadow? Because the shadows were an element, too.
And maybe the reason why something that started as a dare has
endured. You've never given hard-won happiness enough credit,
always chalking it up to luck.

And, yes, luck—that's part of this, too. Because, really, the
whole prospect seemed ill-advised at the outset, the quickness
and timing, but also the simple fact of letting some of the I, I, I slip
from your fist, especially when you'd worked so hard to find it in
the first place, as a daughter and granddaughter, as a mostly good
girl who sensed that the gender game is rigged, and as a grown
woman who came to know it. And then to have regained the I after
filing divorce papers on a winter day in the courthouse that faces a
small-town casino where people win sometimes but mostly walk
away with less than they brought and sometimes more than they
can afford to lose. The aftermath means untangling one life from
another, means confessing to family and friends and banks and the
DMV that you have your old name again (and who knew you'd
have missed it?). So, it seems like a gamble to give up some of the
I for *you*. But then you come to understand the paradox that was
probably illuminated in your friends' more traditional marriage
vows that you only half heard while you waited for the violins and
cake: that you can become more of yourself beside a second person.

And that, from the other person's perspective, you're *their* second person—the accomplice, the sidekick, the secondary character in the story told from their point of view as they become more of themselves across a lifetime, too.

The middle-middle? It's this moment. In his pink chair across the room, he doesn't look different except for the silver stripe in his beard, something that seemed to manifest overnight two years ago when you both woke up and there it was: a straight line of white to match the single white eyelash he's had since you met him. But surely he must have changed more than that. *You* have—so much so that the woman in the yellow tank top seems like someone you dreamed. Last week, when you applied mascara in the passenger side mirror as he drove through your neighborhood, you said aloud almost by accident, "When did we get older?" to which he replied, "We're fine." Because it's a trick how you think you're making a life only to see that you've already made it.

What you've made? In the middle-middle, the weight of it feels heavy and precious. In the middle-middle, it's things like this: he calls you from the hospital across the country where his dad is terminally ill and you're in a blizzard walking the dog across a frozen bridge, heavy tree boughs arcing above your head and the only sounds along the miraculously untouched paths are of snow settling and the dog's soft pant and his voice through the phone. You're the only people remaining in the world: *Holy shit, this is love,* you think and you can practically feel the big clock ticking which means this might be as good as it gets and, finally, what more could you need? But it's also this: the other night, in total darkness, two a.m., he woke you up to offer a glass of cold water because he said you looked thirsty in your sleep, and you *were* thirsty, actually, and so you sat up to drink it, to talk nonsense inside the dark for a moment you'll barely remember before placing the half-full glass on the nightstand.

One time, because you talk about writing as much as you talk about anything else, he tells you that second person is his least favorite point of view. You tell him it's one of your favorites. You're not just being contrary: it's intimate somehow, despite the lack of I, like a pact you're making with a reader, a whisper in their ear. So you wonder if, when you tell him you're writing this essay in second person—this one with the light—he'll say it's a bad idea, too annoying or over-the-top. When you mention it, you say it from the sofa where you're typing on your ancient laptop with the frayed cord and he's walking around, playing his bass, lines that will get stuck in your head for days. "Oh," he says, "like in the love poems. The I/you address." You tell him that this isn't that kind of essay, though, that there really isn't any I in it.

Except, of course, it's all I. The second person just makes it easier to turn the bright jewel around in your palm. And although this essay isn't a love poem, a direct address to the *you*, maybe you did mean to talk to readers all along. You know that the particulars of this story—red truck, scorched Mojave, cowboy shirt with the frayed hem—aren't their love-story particulars: they have their own weathered maps and soundtracks and moving boxes and beds in which they breathe and curve against another in the dark. You suppose that, for some, a beginning waits just beyond their sightline. For others, you're pretty sure they've come to the end, that the clock stopped and now their phone remains silent as they walk their dog through frozen woods. You think, they're in the early-middle or middle-middle or late-middle. Not writing down each day but living it instead. Love so ordinary that it's extraordinary. *I see it*, you want to say to them, *your common, rare thing*.

TITLES OF ESSAYS
I DIDN'T WRITE

The Essay in Which My Family Doesn't Appear

Who Knew a River Could Be So Silent?

There Is More to Life Than Death

I Don't Know the Answer to Guns, But I Know Guns Won't Tell
You the Answer

An Essay in Which I Caught a Fish Once but Regretted It on Shore

The Bands That Taught Us What We Needed to Know

How to Have Faith in Ghosts

Beyond Late-Stage Capitalism, or If You're Lost in California You
Can Always Look for the Sea

Art History: The Women and Siblings

Why I'm Adjunct Teaching, Again

American Dream Dictionary (2021 Ed.)

The Sounds of Trees from My Youth

Things You Don't Have to Be Taught

THINGS YOU DON'T HAVE
TO BE TAUGHT, 1982

Dust devils trouble the yard, toss tumbleweeds. They frazzle the chickens and the furious rooster who'll chase you if he doesn't like your look. One morning I walk outside to find my grandparents and parents slaughtering them. The four move together, their hands working blades and buckets of water. It's a shock to witness this, like the first time I watched my mom clean fish in Frances's sink. Nature is cruel enough without us: hens will peck their own to death. But even as a kid, I know about perspective. How the slit silver trout bellies beneath the faucet shimmer like sequins on a dress. How the down floating in the morning sunlight suggests magic, angels even, their heavy evidence at my feet.

TRANSCRIPT: HAZARDS

BILL DRESSER: We were about four houses from the 405 freeway. And we were there before the freeway was built. After they built that freeway it got pretty noisy, traffic . . . and invariably a car would go through the fence and end up on our street.

FRANCES DRESSER: Not close to our house but the end of the block.

BD: I remember one place. I think it was sailors in the car.

FD: Oh, yeah.

BD: And the police came out and the sailors took off. The car's still sitting there. And the sailors ended up walking away from it.

ASHLEY FARMER: I wonder what exit that's by on the 405 because I probably still drive that.

BD: Artesia Boulevard. Off-ramp there at Artesia Boulevard. Also, the Los Angeles River ran right down through there. It almost paralleled the freeway.

AF: What was the river like back then?

FD: [*Laughs.*] About like it is now. When it rained, it flooded, though.

BD: People wondered why the hell they'd build a big river like that, and just a little trickle of water running down it. But when you got a really a good flood with water coming down out of the mountains and everything else, I'd be going to work there and cross that river and see mattresses and furniture and everything else floating down the river.

FD: We'd stand on the hill where we lived and see this stuff. [*Laughs.*] I remember there was this chicken riding on a table.

AF: You'd sail out of Alamitos Bay?

FD: That's later on. That's when we moved to Long Beach. And we were there for the earthquake.

AF: Which earthquake?

FD: Was it renowned? Renowned enough for me to stay out of school.

BD: It wasn't renowned. It was the Los Angeles earthquake that happened in the '30s. And my school was demolished. And I think yours was, wasn't it?

FD: No school!

BD: And it was centralized pretty much around Long Beach. You could look up at like an eight- or ten-story building or apartment and half of it was gone and you'd see bathtubs and toilets and different furniture sitting there but the wall would be gone.

FD: That earthquake was scary. You know, our house in LA was built on a hill so half of the house was up here and half was down below. Christ, we were afraid to sleep in there after that earthquake. And then my dad let us sleep in the living room on the floor because our house, you could see where it was put together in the middle. So we got to sleep on the living room floor when that was happening.

BD: That was a funny thing: you had that earthquake and then you had tremors and they could almost predict when you was going to have another one. We'd walk outside and wait and then have that shake and then go back in the house. You don't remember that I'll bet, do you?

FD: I do, too.

NO ONE IS WAITING

A pandemic arrives, but I still have a birthday. How can this be? Early April 2020: bees buzz in the redbuds, birds chirp on the branches. We don't yet know all this disaster will bring.

I have the day off from work, which now occurs from my laptop in our tiny back room. There's nowhere to be, so I let my dog drag me where he wants to walk. Texts vibrate in my pocket. Roses bloom in electric peach, deep scarlet, rich, buttery yellow—they spill onto the sidewalk. When Ryan's dad died last year, flowers filled the funeral home, more than we could carry, and I'd hoped the abandoned bouquets lived a little longer at the next funeral in that same low-lit room or appeared at someone else's rainy graveside service. Maybe Ryan's dad watches this pandemic from a heavenly casino boat, smoking a Winston and shaking his head until he hits another row of cherries and forgets Earth again. "He'd hate this," we say of him but also of Bill and Frances and friends who've died this year or in the past—the uncomfortable comfort of knowing that our dearly departed wouldn't enjoy this catastrophe.

Back home, from my sofa, I watch a FedEx guy deliver a box: it's from a bakery that makes special cakes and cookies, which Ryan has ordered for my birthday—a gift that feels at once decadent and frivolous and thoughtful during this moment of uncertainty. I hear the driver leave it on the porch, then watch him walk down the steps toward his truck. He's nearly there when he stops to pick up a snail. He cradles it in his gloved hands and carries it to a ring

NO ONE IS WAITING

NO ONE IS WAITING

of red tulips that grow in our front yard. He considers the two flowers nearest to him and places the snail inside the bigger one. This moment of tenderness—this very minor mercy—seems to mean something on a day that is both melancholy and surreal.

Maybe because I already miss the wider world, I share what happened in a tweet, just the facts of the moment: driver, snail, tulip. The tweet gets liked and retweeted by a few friends, then notifications accumulate: someone makes a joke about *snail mail* while another person declares the driver a hero and salutes all essential workers. Several people say, "Thank you for this" or "I do this same thing, too!" or some version of "Can I get this guy's number?" An artist makes an illustrated comic of the moment, the man in his gloves placing the snail inside the flower. Someone tags the VP of FedEx Canada and writes, "I thought you might like this." Later on, the official FedEx Twitter account replies, "Sometimes it's the little things."

But not everyone has a positive take, like the stranger who posts a GIF of a snail shriveling in salt or the throngs who inform me that snails kill tulips—people who admonish the FedEx guy for dooming the flowers and who point out that I'm obviously not a gardener. Some people joke: If this driver is so careful, why do *my* deliveries show up damaged? One woman claims "they steal packages" to which another jokes, "Look, if a snail can get away with your package before you catch up that might be your problem"—a reply that gets thousands of likes. Others accuse me of being a corporate plant or part of a propaganda stunt, and others still wonder if this moment even happened, how I managed to so clearly see something that quick and tiny from my living room window. (Our yard is small.)

That evening, Ryan and I walk along a path near our house

where children have left chalk drawings of panda bears and hopeful messages and avant-garde hopscotch boards, while the snail approaches some eighty thousand likes and eight thousand retweets. Back home, I turn the notifications off to eat cookies and watch Netflix with Ryan and FaceTime with my mom on the back porch. If I imagine hard enough, this day could be any day in the old world, like the last ordinary one when my colleague and I snatched our laptops from the office we share, both of us thinking we'd return soon. But that was exactly one month ago and now the sky is a dramatic, inky wash of pink above the Oquirrh Mountains with darkness rolling in on white clouds.

\/◄

By the time the sweets are gone, the snail is too, the tulip has died, and the tweet has become a meme shared by online magazines and Facebook groups. A close friend sees it in her Instagram feed, texts me, "Is this you??" Like with the original tweet, people are divided. To some, it's a fragment of kindness at a time when anything positive offers a split second of distraction. To others, it ignores a brutal reality. Which I understand, of course: it seems there's no end to the ways that tenderness infiltrates suffering, and vice versa. At any given moment, there are countless combinations of darkness and light.

\/◄

Certainty is a daydream: we're certain only until something upends our reality to prove that we can't be certain, that we never could be in the first place. When my sister called six years ago to tell me about my grandparents and the shooting, I felt, in addition to anguish and shock, a kind of warm, subtle awe at the fact that I had never seen it coming. How could something so unpredictable occur? After all, I'd thought about my grandparents getting older, about what their eventual passing might mean and, maybe selfishly, how it would affect me. It felt straightforward that I would miss them. Yet never in that preemptive grief could I have conjured their scenario. Which mirrors this April moment, too: the world has changed and I'm reminded again that more can happen than what I might predict.

Time loops. Like the public stories and comments about my grandparents' incident—the mug shot, the DA's verdict, other writers' articles, random strangers' perspectives—my birthday echoes in the online account of a singular moment, about a flower and creature that multiplied virtually but are already dust, that died right after my birthday. Days tick forward but we get up, sit in the same spot for a Zoom call or prepare to do essential work, stay inside except to walk our dogs, call our friends, nod to neighbors watering plants on their porches or taking out their trash, each from within their own shocked dream, remarking some version of *This is history right now* or simply *Strange times.* Only the weather shifting from early spring to midspring signifies days cranking forward. We exist in the perpetual present, inside seconds, in the aftershocks. We exist on the internet where our impressions and presence are somehow both immortal and fleeting.

Every so often, a new notification lights up my phone, someone liking the offhand tweet and extending its life by a miniscule margin. The tulips are shot—they don't last long. Honestly, I didn't even know I had them: I've lived in this house for less than a year, so the first day the shoots sprung from the ground, they came as a minor surprise folded into the larger surprise of what would be a new reality. And there's this: I'd always believed that for bulbs to grow, a person must plant new ones each year, that each flower only bloomed once. Walking through Syracuse, where tulips of every color erupt after harsh winter—these wild celebrations springing from the ground—I was in awe of the collective dedication it took to make them grow. Who were these people that planted entire hillsides full of them? Who went to such hard work for just a week or two of blooms? All of that care for a single flower? It made me love strangers every time I saw a daffodil.

I cut what was left of the tulips down the other day, snipped them off with regular scissors because I haven't bought gardening shears. The strangers who said I know nothing about flowers are right, and so I don't know if this was a good move, if the flowers will even return. No one is waiting for them. Maybe they were just a one-time phenomenon—something beautiful that arrived, made their brief impression, and then disappeared. It's enough that they were here.

BILL AND FRANCES DRESSER, OUTSIDE PIOCHE, NEVADA (1950)

APPENDIX

LETTER TO THE
PUBLIC DEFENDER

May 6th, 2015
To Whom It May Concern,

My name is Ashley Farmer and I'm the granddaughter of William
L. Dresser and the late Frances L. Dresser. As their oldest grandchild, and one who was fortunate enough to live near them for a
good number of years, I've always been very close to them both.
When I was a kid, they were huge-hearted, generous, and devoted
grandparents: they babysat me, took me fishing and camping,
encouraged me in school, and spent countless hours with me and
my siblings.

Some of my happiest moments in life were in their company.
Moreover, they've been influential in the best of ways: honest,
upright, empathetic, supportive during challenging times, generous with their attention, and thoughtful with their guidance. I've
looked up to them for more reasons than I could list here.

As an adult, I've come to love them in a new way and I've spent a
great deal of time with them over the past decade. Multiple times
per year I've been able to travel and visit them, to sit again on
the porch of the house they built together, and talk to them. I've
recorded many of these conversations on afternoons where I'd ask

them to recount stories about their families and how they met and what life was like for them as they started their family. In fact, just two weeks before my grandmother went to the hospital, I had several days to visit with them and record them as they talked to one another and told parts of their stories. I'm so grateful for this. I listen to the recordings when I want to reflect on how happy they've been together and how much they mean to me.

I wasn't there when my grandmother had her accident, but I was on the phone with my mom, Cindy Farmer, in the weeks that followed, getting the hopeless, gut-wrenching updates that weren't really updates at all because my grandmother's situation was so bleak. The last time I spoke to my grandmother, my mom held the phone up so my grandma could try to speak to me. Her words were nearly unintelligible, but she tried to utter a hopeful phrase she used to say in the past. It made my heart break because it was clear just how utterly hopeless things were, but I could tell she didn't want me to worry or know just how much she was suffering. It was all too clear, though.

While I wasn't there when she passed, I was, however, at my mom's/grandfather's home the day my grandfather was released from jail. I have always known my grandfather to be very upright, moral, a model citizen, and a very steady and constant person; no one could have anticipated his actions. But I was so grateful to have the chance to hug him again and to spend more time with him, even in all of the grief our family shared.

While I never would have imagined that this turn of events could happen in my family, I have within me an understanding of them.

I know how deeply my grandparents loved each other and how neither of them could have stood to see the other suffer. My grandmother was strong-willed, vibrant, curious about the world, charming, perceptive, very funny, and smart. She loved nature. She loved to tap her feet to good music and hold her great-grandchildren close to her. It is impossible to imagine her living without those pleasures, without her basic human dignity, and in a state of constant physical pain. I know her well enough to say that I very strongly believe she would not have wanted to.

A lot has changed for me since my grandmother's death. I've become more compassionate to those who are suffering. I understand that bad things can quite suddenly happen to good people. Every day I think about how extremely difficult it would be if I were to find myself in either my grandfather's or grandmother's position: without hope, even if you're surrounded by the most supportive, loving family that would do anything to make things better for you. But for everything that has changed, some things have not: my love for my grandparents, my belief in their love for each other, my respect for them both, and how deeply, deeply I value them.

With thanks sincerely,

Ashley Farmer

MOTION TO DISMISS

Case No.   14 CR 00086 1C

Dept. No.   II

IN THE JUSTICE COURT OF CARSON TOWNSHIP

IN AND FOR CARSON CITY, STATE OF NEVADA

STATE OF NEVADA,

        Plaintiff,

v.

WILLIAM LYLE DRESSER,

        Defendant.

MOTION TO DISMISS

COMES NOW, the STATE OF NEVADA, by and through ████████████ District Attorney in and for Carson City, State of Nevada, and hereby moves this Honorable Court for an order dismissing the *Criminal Complaint* filed in this case on January 22, 2014.

This *Motion* is made pursuant to NRS 178.552 and NRS 178.554 and is based on the points and authorities set forth below and all pleadings and papers heretofore filed in this case.

DATED this 18th day of June, 2015.

CARSON CITY DISTRICT ATTORNEY

By: ████████████

District Attorney

Office of the District Attorney
Carson City, Nevada
885 East Musser St., Suite 2030, Carson City, Nevada 89701
Tel: (775) 887-2072 Fax: (775) 887-2329

1

POINTS AND AUTHORITIES

I. SUMMARY

The prosecution of this matter would serve no worthy purpose.

II. FACTUAL BACKGROUND[1]

In early January 2014, Frances Dresser fell in her home. Mrs. Dresser was 86 years old at the time, and her fall resulted in significant injuries, including severe spinal cord damage. Mrs. Dresser spent the next two weeks at the Carson Tahoe Regional Medical Center as medical personnel diagnosed and treated her injuries. Ultimately, doctors settled upon a disheartening prognosis. Due to her advanced age and other issues, surgery was not a viable option. Mrs. Dresser would remain a quadripalegic for the remainder of her life, requiring virtually round-the-clock care.

On January 18, 2014, Carson Tahoe medical staff met with the Dresser family at the hospital to deliver this information. The staff recommended the Dressers find a suitable nursing home for the placement of Mrs. Dresser upon her discharge.

William Dresser is Frances Dresser's husband. They were married July 12, 1950. He was 88 years old and had been married to Mrs. Dresser for 63 years when Mrs. Dresser fell and went to the hospital. Mr. Dresser attended the meeting on January 18 and heard the account of his wife's condition and the dismal prognosis.

Cindy Farmer is the daughter of Mr. and Mrs. Dresser. About a year before Mrs. Dresser's fall, Mr. Dresser asked Ms. Farmer to move in with Mr. and Mrs. Dresser as health issues were making it difficult for them to live without assistance. During that time, Mrs.

[1] The factual representations contained herein are based upon a review of all police and forensic reports, witness statements, interviews with Mr. Dresser and witnesses, photographs, medical records from Carson Tahoe Regional Healthcare and Renown Health, letters provided by the Dresser family and Mr. Dresser's urologist, consultation with a physician and prison officials, and media accounts relating to this case. To the extent there is any inconsistency among those sources, and there is little, the factual representations herein reflect where the balance of the reliable evidence lies.

Office of the District Attorney
Carson City, Nevada
885 East Musser St., Suite 2030, Carson City, Nevada 89701
Tel: (775) 887-2072 Fax: (775) 887-2129

1

Dresser frequently fell, but managed to avoid any significant injury. However, her fall on January 7 was different, and Mrs. Dresser seemed to immediately realize that. As they were waiting for emergency assistance, Mrs. Dresser told her husband, "I really did it this time," and as they travelled in the ambulance, Mrs. Dresser asked her daughter, "Cindy, I'm paralyzed, aren't I?" Cindy responded that she "hoped not." Mrs. Dresser then said, "I want to commit suicide."

Mrs. Dresser's two week hospital stay was demoralizing. She was unable to tolerate solid food restricting her to a liquid diet, and according to family members:

- Mrs. Dresser was "absolutely miserable."
- "She lost all interest in everything around her."
- "She lost everything she could possibly do or enjoy."
- "Seeing her deteriorate physically and mentally was awful."
- Mrs. Dresser suffered "excruciating" and "continuous" pain.

On several occasions throughout her hospitalization, Mrs. Dresser expressed a desire to end her life, and on one occasion she attempted to reject her medication and liquid food in an apparent effort toward that end.[2]

After the January 18 meeting between medical staff and the Dresser family, culminating in the determination that Mrs. Dresser's condition would never improve and she required placement in a nursing home, Mrs. Dresser stated again that she did not want to live any longer—she preferred to die.

---

[2] Most poignantly, the Dressers' eldest grandchild captured the situation as follows:

My grandmother was strong-willed, vibrant, curious about the world, charming, perceptive, very funny, and smart. She loved nature. She loved to tap her feet to good music and hold her great-grandchildren close to her. It is impossible to imagine her living without those pleasures, without her basic human dignity, and in a state of constant physical pain. I know her well enough to say that I very strongly believe she would not have wanted to.

Office of the District Attorney
Carson City, Nevada
885 East Musser St., Suite 2030, Carson City, nevada 89701
Tel. (775) 887-2072 Fax: (775) 887-2129

2

1   Mr. Dresser spent that night considering what to do. On the morning of January 19, Mr.

2 Dresser made his decision. He went to a pawn shop, purchased a handgun, and loaded it

3 with four rounds. He drove to the hospital and went inside with the gun concealed. He

4 walked past the nurse's station outside his wife's hospital room. He went into the hospital

5 room and saw that Mrs. Dresser was sleeping. He kissed her. And at 11:29 a.m. on January

6

7 19, 2014, he shot her once in her chest.[3] Frances Dresser died a short time later.

8   Mr. Dresser had loaded four rounds into the handgun because he planned to shoot

9 himself after he shot his wife.[4] But the gun jammed as he tried to reload the chamber. As

10 medical staff and others rushed into Mrs. Dresser's room after hearing the gunshot, Mr.

11 Dresser did not threaten them with the firearm, and he did not obstruct in any way their efforts

12 to save his wife. He only pleaded with them to "please let her die; she wants to die." Mr.

13 Dresser was subsequently arrested—the first arrest of his life—and charged with one count of

14 Open Murder with the Use of a Deadly Weapon, a category A felony as defined by NRS

15 193.165, 200.010, 200.030.[5] Following Mr. Dresser's arrest, he appeared before this Court on

16 January 23, 2014, at which time the Nevada State Public Defender's Office was appointed as

17

18 his counsel.

19   Prior to these events, in July 2008, Mr. Dresser was diagnosed with inoperable high-

20 grade prostate cancer. His current treatment involves quarterly Lupron Depot injections at an

21 average cost of $16,000 per dose. His urologist reports that Mr. Dresser is beginning to show

22 signs of resistance to that treatment which will require modification of Mr. Dresser's treatment

23 plan to include the administration of Xtandi at an anticipated cost of $6,000 to $8,000 per

24 month. Even more expensive chemotherapy treatments are predicted once Xtandi loses

25 efficacy.

26

27

28

[3] Due to her paralysis, Mrs. Dresser felt no pain resulting from the gunshot.
[4] Mr. Dresser told the lead detective in the case, "I put four bullets in the gun, and I figured two for her and two for me."

Office of the District Attorney
Carson City, Nevada
885 East Musser st., Suite 2030, Carson City, Nevada 89701
Tel: (775) 887-2072 Fax: (775) 887-2129

3

III. DISCUSSION

The concept of prosecutorial discretion is well established in the common law.[6] In Nevada, the power is codified at NRS 178.554 which provides that a District Attorney "may by leave of court file a dismissal of an indictment, information or complaint and the prosecution shall thereupon terminate." The decision to move for dismissal in this case has been made after careful consideration of many factors, the most important of which are discussed below.

A. NATURE OF THE CRIME

Under Nevada law, a "willful, deliberate, and premeditated killing" is first degree murder.[7] "Willfulness is the intent to kill."[8] "Deliberation is the process of determining upon a course of action to kill as a result of thought, including weighing the reasons for and against the action and considering the consequences of the action."[9] "Premeditation is a design, a determination to kill, distinctly formed in the mind by the time of the killing."[10] The evidence recounted above is essentially undisputed and strongly indicates that Mr. Dresser intended, deliberated upon, and premeditated the killing of Mrs. Dresser. While those answers are clear, they do not address the ultimate question in this case.

Since there has been law, there has been recognition of the singular nature of murder as a criminal act. William Blackstone provided an early, if not the original, legal definition of the criminal offense of murder, together with its distinctive element: malice aforethought.[11] The quintessential term of art, over the centuries, the concept of "malice aforethought" has evolved to apply in some circumstances which involve neither "malice" nor "aforethought" as

\\\\

\\\\

---

[6] See *Criminal Complaint* (Jan. 22, 2014).
[6] See *Sandy v. Fifth Jud. Dist. Ct.*, 113 Nev. 435, 439-40, 935 P.2d 1148, 1150-51 (1997); *Discretionary Authority of the Prosecutor* (1977).
[7] *Byford v. State*, 116 Nev. 215, 236, 994 P.2d 700, 713 (2000).
[8] *Byford*, 116 Nev. at 236, 994 P.2d at 714.
[9] *Id.*
[10] *Byford*, 116 Nev. at 237, 994 P.2d at 714.
[11] *Compare* Blackstone, Sir William, IV *Commentaries on the Laws of England* at 500 ("Murder is 'when a person of sound memory and discretion, unlawfully killeth any reasonable creature in being, and under the king's peace, with malice aforethought, either express or implied.'") *with* NRS 200.010(1) ("Murder is the unlawful killing of a human being ... [w]ith malice aforethought, either express or implied.")

Office of the District Attorney
Carson City, Nevada
885 East Musser St., Suite 2030, Carson City, Nevada 89701
Tel: (775) 887-2072 Fax: (775) 887-2129

4

1   those words are customarily understood. Nonetheless, the *sine qua non* of murder survives.

2   Some element of **evil** must drive the murderer's act to end another's life.[12]

3   That insoluble bond between evil and murder is what makes this case so difficult at first

4   glance and so simple upon reflection. William Lyle Dresser killed his wife, but he is not a

5   murderer. He saw his wife of 63 years immobile in a hospital bed, paralyzed from the neck

6   down, suffering with no hope of improvement, facing a short existence not remotely

7   resembling a life she cared to live. So he ended that life. And he ended that suffering.

8   Whether that decision was morally right or wrong and whether it was even his to make

9   is obviously the subject of solemn debate in our society. Some, including Mrs. Dresser's

10   family, consider his decision the ultimate act of compassion for his wife. Others, no doubt, will

11   believe it arrogant, impetuous, even selfish. But no reasonable person would consider the act

12   in this case to be evil.

13   **B. VICTIM'S WISHES**

14   When evaluating alternatives in prosecuting a violent crime, the principal consideration

15   of most prosecutors is the victim's wishes. When a victim expresses a desired outcome, the

16   Carson City District Attorney's Office directs its efforts toward that outcome provided it is

17   consistent with justice and strategically and legally achievable. In this case, the evidence

18   indicates:

19   •   After her fall, Mrs. Dresser expressed a desire to end her life on multiple

20   occasions;

21   •   Those closest to Mrs. Dresser, her children and grandchildren, are in universal

22   and uniform agreement that Mrs. Dresser did not want to live in her condition;

23   and

24   •   Mrs. Dresser's family does not wish Mr. Dresser to be prosecuted.

25   I am satisfied that if she were able to express it, Mrs. Dresser would affirm that she would not

26   wish for her husband to be prosecuted in this case.

27   [12] *See* NRS 200.020. (Express malice is "that deliberate intention unlawfully to take away the life of a fellow creature," and malice is implied when "the circumstances of the killing show an **abandoned and malignant**

28   **heart**." (emphasis added)).

Office of the District Attorney
Carson City, Nevada
885 East Musser St., Suite 2030, Carson City, Nevada 89701
Tel: (775) 887-2072 Fax: (775) 867-2129

5

C. COST/BENEFIT

The objective of justice, not economics, has prompted the decision in this case. But it would be irresponsible to ignore the substantial financial repercussions to taxpayers which would result from the prosecution and incarceration of Mr. Dresser.

1. Trial Costs

Murder trials exact significant costs on taxpayers. A recent study commissioned by the Nevada Legislature concluded that the average cost of a non-capital murder case is $233,000 for trial and appeal proceedings.[13] Moreover, there is reason to believe that the trial and appellate costs required in this case would even exceed that figure.

Because the material factual circumstances in this case are clear, a trial would likely focus on Mr. Dresser's mental state. At taxpayer expense, expert witnesses would be retained by both the prosecution and defense to evaluate Mr. Dresser's mental condition, consult with counsel concerning their conclusions and to testify at the trial and preliminary proceedings. Experts of this type command large fees. These costs, likely tens of thousands of dollars, would be over and above the costs normally associated with a murder case.

2. Incarceration Costs

Further, depending on how long he lives, the substantial costs implicated in the prosecution and defense of Mr. Dresser's case could be microscopic compared to the costs required to incarcerate[14] him if he was convicted. On average, Nevada spends about $20,000 per year to incarcerate an inmate.[15] That figure is higher when an inmate is elderly and higher still when an inmate is a person with special medical needs. Mr. Dresser is both, and that alone would significantly elevate the financial burden of putting him in prison. But that's not the half of it.

\\\\

[13] See Legislative Auditor, *Performance Audit Fiscal Costs of the Death Penalty 2014* at 11 (Nov. 17, 2014) (http://www.leg.state.nv.us/Division/Audit/Full/BE2014/Costs%20of%20Death%20Penalty,%20LA14-25.%20Full.pdf) (last visited June 15, 2015).
[14] If convicted of murder, Mr. Dresser could not be sentenced to probation. See NRS 176A.100 (1)(a).
[15] See Nevada Department of Corrections, *Stat Facts* (Mar. 27, 2015) http://doc.nv.gov/uploadedFiles/docnvgov/content/About/Statistics/WFS/FactSheetsWeekly03272015.pdf (last visited June 17, 2015).

Office of the District Attorney
Carson City, Nevada
885 East Musser St., Suite 2030, Carson City, Nevada 89701
Tel.: (775) 887-2072 Fax: (775) 887-2129

6

1   The cost of Mr. Dresser's prostate cancer treatment is enormous and growing. His
2 current Lupron injections cost $64,000 annually. When he transitions to Xtrandi, the yearly
3 cost will increase to somewhere between $72,000 and $96,000. The inevitable chemotherapy
4 will be even more. Presently, those costs are the responsibility of Mr. Dresser, most likely
5 covered by Medicare. However, neither Medicaid nor Medicare cover these costs if Mr.
6 Dresser becomes an inmate of the Nevada Department of Corrections.[16] Nevada taxpayers
7 would pay these costs.

8   In other cases, costs like these are justified by the public benefits associated with a
9 conviction. Not in this one.

10   **D. COUNTERVAILING CONCERNS**

11   Nevertheless, this is a hard case. Two factors make it especially so.

12   First, the method by which Mr. Dresser decided to end Mrs. Dresser's life is extremely
13 troubling. Introduction of a firearm into this community's hospital could have transformed this
14 event from an isolated tragedy into a widespread catastrophe in the blink of an eye. Mr.
15 Dresser's reckless decision placed innocent lives in danger.

16   There is some comfort to be taken in the fact that this did not materialize. Mr. Dresser
17 obtained access to Mrs. Dresser's private room without the firearm being detected. He shot
18 Mrs. Dresser without endangering anyone else. And as emergency medical personnel
19 responded to Mrs. Dresser and law enforcement personnel responded to the scene, he did
20 nothing to place any of them in physical danger.[17] None of the hospital staff or other
21 responders involved in the incident report any adverse psychological consequences and none
22 have required ongoing counseling services.

23   The second concern has to do with deterrence. Deterrence is an important objective of
24 the criminal justice system.[18] A community expresses its moral preferences through the law
25 which imposes sanctions designed to influence the behavior of community members. In the

26 [16] See 42 CFR Ch. IV Subchapter B §411.8; 42 CFR Ch. IV Subchapter C §435.1009.
27 [17] Obscured in this event is the valiance of the hospital's staff. Without hesitation, Nurse Nancy Baltes and Nursing Assistant Fernando Platero rushed into Mrs. Dresser's room immediately after hearing the gunshot and provided aid to Mrs. Dresser even as Mr. Dresser continued to hold the firearm.
28 [18] See e.g., Carter v. State, 98 Nev. 331, 334, 647 P.2d 374, 376 (1982).

Office of the District Attorney
Carson City, Nevada
885 East Musser St., Suite 2030, Carson City, Nevada 89701
Tel. (775) 887-2072 Fax (775) 887-2129

7

1 absence of a sanction, the deterrent effect of a law may be diminished on the assumption that
2 the community tolerates the behavior at issue. As applicable here, it is distressing to consider
3 that some might interpret the dismissal of this case to mean that any instance of conduct
4 which might fall within the general rubric of "assisted suicide" will evade prosecution in Carson
5 City.

6   Of course, this is not the case. The dismissal of this matter is based entirely on the
7 virtually unique circumstances of this particular case. A single variation would change the
8 analysis and could change the result. To be clear, no general policy decision legitimizing
9 "assisted suicide" has been made or is intended in this dismissal. A policy level decision of
10 that kind is the province of the Legislature.

11   While it is not possible to entirely resolve these troublesome concerns, I have
12 concluded that they are outweighed by the other considerations discussed which favor
13 dismissal.

14 **IV. CONCLUSION**

15   For the foregoing reasons, it is respectfully requested that this Court dismiss the
16 *Criminal Complaint* filed in this case on January 22, 2014 and vacate further proceedings.

17   DATED this 18th day of June, 2015.

18   CARSON CITY DISTRICT ATTORNEY

19

20   By:

21   District Attorney

22

23

24

25

26

27

28

8

Office of the District Attorney
Carson City, Nevada
885 East Musser St., Suite 2030, Carson City, Nevada 89701
Tel: (775) 887-2072 Fax: (775) 887-2129

1

CERTIFICATE OF SERVICE

2   I certify that I am an employee of the Office of the Carson City District Attorney and that

3   on this 18th day of June, 2015, I caused to be served a copy of the foregoing by depositing for

4   hand delivery via Reno-Carson Messenger Service a true and correct copy of said document

5   addressed to:

6

7

8

9

10

11

12

13

14

15

16

17

18

19

20

21

22

23

24

25

26

27

28

SOURCES

Berman, David. "Self-Portrait at 28." In *Actual Air*, 54–61. New York: Open City Books, 1999.

Berman, David. "About the Party." *The Believer* 7, October 1, 2003. https://believermag.com/about-the-party/.

Thompson, Hunter S. Illustrated by Ralph Steadman. *Fear and Loathing in Las Vegas: A Savage Journey to the Heart of the American Dream*. New York: Random House, 1972. Reprinted as a Second Vintage Book Edition. New York: Vintage, 1998.

Vredenburg, Jason. "What Happens in Vegas: Hunter S. Thompson's Political Philosophy." *Journal of American Studies* 47, no. 1 (February 2013): 149–170.

Ziegler, Alan. "Love at First Sight." In *The Swan Song of Vaudeville: Tales and Takes*. Omaha: Zoo Press. Online at Minnesota Public Radio's *The Writer's Almanac*, March 28, 2006. https://writersalmanac.publicradio.org/index.php%3Fdate=2006%252F03%252F28.html.

ACKNOWLEDGMENTS

My enormous gratitude to Sarah Gorham of Sarabande Books for her editorial brilliance and generosity. Thank you also to Sarabande's incredible team, including Kristen Miller, Joanna Englert, Danika Isdahl, Lacey Trautwein, and Natalie Wollenzien. I'm grateful to Alban Fischer for his stunning design work and Emma Aprile for her copyediting expertise. Thank you all for bringing this book to life.

I'm grateful to Gina Nutt, Justin St. Germain, and Michelle Latiolais: thank you for your inspiration and generous words. Thank you to Roxane Gay for publishing an excerpt from this collection in *Gay Magazine* and to Laura June Topolsky for her thoughtful edits. Thank you also to *Ninth Letter* and contest judge Elissa Washuta for selecting my work for their 2018 literary award for nonfiction. I'm indebted to my amazing teachers and mentors: Christopher Kennedy, Michael Burkard, Mary Karr, George Saunders, Bruce Smith, Brooks Haxton, David Treuer, Christine Schutt, Paul Griner, Jeffrey Skinner, Ron Whitehead, Wayne Fowler, and Martha Clark, among others.

Deep appreciation to Abraham Smith, Alan Grostephan, the Baringer house, Carroll Beauvais, Christy Crutchfield, Claire Krüeger, Gavin Grace, Gene Kwak, Jeffrey Bean, John Colasacco, John Kim, John Wang, Lauren Swan, María Korol, Mel Bosworth, Nadxieli Nieto, Ryan Daly, Ryan Hume, the Snarlin' Yarns, and

Wax Fang. Endless gratitude to the Syracuse writing community, as well as the creative spaces and friendships I've been lucky to be a part of in Louisville, Long Beach, Irvine, and Salt Lake City.

To Melodi and the women: my heartfelt gratitude. Thank you always to the Dresser, Farmer, LeCount, and Ridge families, as well as relatives and friends inside this book. My huge-hearted thanks to Randie, Katie, Bill E., Holly & John, and Aunt Kelly. To Ryan: per aspera ad astra. Thank you with love to Dennis, Cindy, Brendan, Cameron, and Mallory. And to William and Frances, out there in the wild beyond.

PUBLICATION CREDITS

Some essays within this collection have appeared in the following publications, in slightly different forms: *Gay Magazine* and *Ninth Letter*.

RYAN RIDGE

ASHLEY FARMER is the author of *The Women, The Farmacist,* and *Beside Myself.* Her essays, poems, and stories can be found in *Gay Magazine, TriQuarterly, The Progressive, Flaunt, Nerve, Gigantic, BuzzFeed, DIAGRAM, Santa Monica Review,* and elsewhere. Ashley has received a *Best American Essays 2019* Notable Essay distinction, *Ninth Letter's* 2018 Literary Award in Creative Nonfiction, the *Los Angeles Review's* 2017 Short Fiction Award, and fellowships from Syracuse University and the Baltic Writing Residency. Ashley holds degrees from the University of Louisville and the Syracuse University Creative Writing MFA Program. She lives in Salt Lake City with the writer Ryan Ridge.

SARABANDE BOOKS is a nonprofit literary press located in Louisville, KY. Founded in 1994 to champion poetry, short fiction, and essay, we are committed to creating lasting editions that honor exceptional writing. For more information, please visit sarabandebooks.org.